HORIZONS CIRCLED

Reflections on My Music

Ernst Krenek. (Fotostudio Pfeifer)

ERNST KRENEK

HORIZONS CIRCLED

Reflections on My Music

With Contributions by WILL OGDON

and JOHN L. STEWART

UNIVERSITY OF CALIFORNIA PRESS

Berkeley / Los Angeles / London / 1974

University of California Press
Berkeley and Los Angeles, California
University of California Press, Ltd.
London, England

ISBN: 0-520-02338-2
Library of Congress Catalog Card Number: 72-89790

Designed by Jim Mennick
Printed in the United States of America

Contents

Preface

Early in 1970 Ernst Krenek took up residence as a Regents Lecturer in John Muir College at the University of California, San Diego. It was, in fact, a happy homecoming.

In recognition of his distinguished career and his contribution to this new branch of the university, he had been appointed an Honorary Fellow of the college when it opened in 1967, and to help us celebrate that brave beginning he had composed and directed the performance of a new work, "Exercises of a Late Hour." Now that he was midway through his seventieth year and once again among old friends and admirers, he used the occasion to look back across five decades of unusual productivity and achievement as composer, teacher, and writer. In four informally delivered but exceptionally rich lectures he looked over a wide landscape of arts, letters, education, politics, wars, exile, neglect, and triumph. Later these lectures were slightly revised to become the essays that form the core of this book. Taking his cue from the title of one of his recent major works (analyzed elsewhere in this volume by Will Ogdon), he calls these essays "Circling My Horizons." Within their great compass there is much to be seen.

But Ernst Krenek was more to us than returning friend and distinguished guest lecturer. He was, in truth, the intellectual and artistic forebear of what has become in but a few years an unusually exciting and adventuresome department of music. I had known Ernst since 1948, and we had kept in touch through the years. Thus, when I was asked to come to UCSD in 1964 and take charge of establishing the arts on this new campus, I at once sought his advice. He recommended that we persuade Will Ogdon to leave Illinois Wesleyan University to become our first chairman of music, which we did. Will had studied composing with Ernst. So had the composer Robert Erickson, who was one of the first advanced students to seek him out after Ernst settled in the country. It seemed only natural when, with Ernst's enthusiastic blessing, Will and I recruited Erickson to help found a music program in which creativity of the highest order would be preeminent.

So it is that Ernst's ideas and example have been part of UCSD almost from its beginning. Naturally we wanted to know more about how these ideas had been shaped, how they had been realized in works that belong among the most daring and accomplished of our time, how they still direct his own continuing creativity and through it so much of our thinking about and response to contemporary music. Of course, what he told us had significance far beyond the felicitous moment of its telling, for Ernst is truly an international figure. Thus, with pride and an awareness of our good fortune in our relationship with him that we share with his admirers everywhere, these special exercises of a late hour.

John L. Stewart

John Muir College
The University of California
San Diego

HORIZONS CIRCLED

Reflections on My Music

A Master Composer and a Foremost Musician of Our Time

by WILL OGDON

I

Although Ernst Krenek has composed, taught, and lived in America for nearly thirty-five years, he continues to enjoy a greater amount of official and professional recognition in Europe. This does not imply a lesser regard for his qualities among American peers, but it does underscore the unfortunate facts of life for a professional musician in America. That Krenek customarily spends a part of each year conducting and lecturing in Europe simply tells us how much more restricted is the professional life of a composer-musician in America, except for its campuses. In Europe a substantial part of Krenek's involvement is related to radio, television, and the opera. It is too well known that mass communications in America offer little or nothing to the serious, creative artist and that our opera—or what there is of it—continues to be more a museum than does European opera. So it is not surprising to find this internationally honored musician from America reversing the brain drain by, to a large extent, earning his living in Europe.

Not entirely, of course. During these American years, Krenek has often been identified with American colleges and universities. Beyond innumerable short-term residencies, his academic association was, primarily, with two American campuses: He instructed at Vassar College in Poughkeepsie, New York, from 1939 to 1942, and went from there to a several-year deanship of Hamline University's arts program in St. Paul, Minnesota.

It could be claimed that America owes the burgeoning of its postwar musical vitality to the many European composers and musicians who, like Krenek, were driven from Europe by Hitler to find refuge in America. Some accepted professorial assignments in America as Krenek did and still others chose not to teach but exerted their influence on a few cosmopolitan areas of the United States where their music was occasionally heard. A remarkable number ended their flight on the California coast in the Los Angeles area.

It took several years longer for Krenek, than it did his colleagues Schoenberg and Stravinsky, to reach Los Angeles. Stopping to fulfill academic obligations to Vassar and Hamline might appear a minor paradox if America's restricted professional opportunities were not kept in mind, for Krenek seemed drawn to the American West and California even in pre-Anschluss Austria.

After abiding the coastal climate of Los Angeles for more than fifteen years, Krenek and his wife Gladys, also an active composer, have sought the desert sun, settling in Palm Springs from where they accept invitations, primarily to American campuses, and assignments and commissions, largely from European opera companies and radio-television stations.

While in residence at the University of California, San Diego, during January and February of 1970, Krenek seemed both amused and pleased that the artist-social circles of Palm Springs had chosen to recognize his presence with an invitation to lecture at the local arts museum. There, Krenek introduced his talk with an anecdote about a personal visit to the island of Corsica. "Who lives in that fine, old white castle up on the hill?" Krenek asked his Corsican guide. "Oh, we don't pay any attention to them. They are upstarts. Why that family didn't settle here until the sixteenth century." Krenek assured his Palm Springs neighbors that he was glad to have escaped the Corsican's fate.

Krenek might well have remembered the story once again when in December of 1971 he listened to the Los Angeles Philharmonic Orchestra perform his *Horizon Circled.* It was the first time since Wallenstein's tenure that this orchestra had played a work of his. Krenek's chamber music, however, has been heard fairly often in Southern California —in Los Angeles, primarily through the sponsorship of the Monday Evening Concerts, and in San Diego, on the campus of the University of California. His chamber opera, *What Price Confidence,* for four singers was presented on several California campuses during the Spring of 1972 allowing one to wonder if the most prolific opera composer in the world will finally hear a major production of a full-length opera in California—or anywhere else in America, for that matter.

II

To introduce Ernst Krenek, the composer I have gathered up for review a rather casual group of compositions whose time of origin spans some forty-five years. Once again I am awed by this composer's wide-ranging diversity of expression and by his consummate display of technique, a rediscovery that, somehow, has helped remind me that Krenek's contemporaries have always regarded him as a composer who kept up with the times. Only once did he attempt, seemingly, to escape. That was in the later 1920s when Krenek tried to revivify the tonal language through a rapprochement with the early Romantic lyricism of Franz Schubert. Even then Krenek could not escape the reality of the future, since Schubert inevitably led him to the technical and, in a broad sense, the expressive regions inhabited by his older Austrian contemporary, Arnold Schoenberg. From that point of contact with Schubert, Krenek's road to Schoenberg's twelve-note method of composition led through the lyric, expressive Austrian tradition as it matured after Beethoven from Schubert through Mahler and on to Schoenberg, Berg, and Webern.

Krenek's habit of inscribing his scores with their dates and places of composition allows me to see that those before me range in time from 1924 to 1970. The earliest of them are Krenek's *Two Suites for Piano* written when the composer was twenty-four years old. The latest is Krenek's *Tape and Double* composed for two pianos and electronic sound in 1969–70. Two other sets of piano pieces are among these scores, the *Basler Massarbeit* for two pianos (1960) and a set of *Eight Piano Pieces* written in 1946.

The 1946 and 1960 sets both include performance instructions and also technical descriptions related to Krenek's personal development of the twelve-tone principle as a compositional resource. In fact, Krenek intended the earlier set as a compendium of row usage, as he had the still earlier *Twelve Piano Pieces* of 1939. The last four of the *Eight Piano Pieces* are particularly significant since they introduce special ways of manipulating the tone row beyond the "classical" manner of Schoenberg. Krenek was interested in the row as a motivic resource in the 1940s and in the row's ability to organize pitch segments as complementary modalities. This postclassical exploration of the row resulted in some very attractive music including Krenek's third and fourth piano sonatas, a monumental setting of the lamentations of Jeremiah, and Krenek's response to the news of Webern's tragic death, an elegy written for string orchestra. Such works antedate Krenek's adaption of the row to other parameters of the musical process as well as his involvement with electronic music, both concerns coming to fruition in the 1950s.

The *Basler Massarbeit* of 1960 is also a compendium, this time of Krenek's serial way of structuring time in the image of the row's note relationships. As the composer tells us in the frontispiece to the publication, "The numerical values of the series are the basis for the measurement, division, succession, and proportional combination of the time spans to be found in the pieces, and for deciding the number of notes to be allotted to each such time span."

Only this 1960 set is rhythmically experimental enough to call for instructions regarding performance of the time structure. Krenek's performing instructions for the earlier eight pieces needed to be cautionary only. The composer could assume that his music's phrasing, its dynamics, touches and pedaling were relying on a conventionally trained musician with a rather normal keyboard technique at his disposal. Beyond the temporal synchronization problems in the *Basler Massarbeit,* there were certain unusual keyboard techniques that needed explaining, such as striking a key sharply and then releasing it only to silently depress it at the same time the right pedal is depressed.

But by the time of *Tape and Double* Krenek seemed to shift his interest to the exploration of piano sound. Constructivist rhythmic serialization is not much in evidence and neither are the hazards of complicated time synchronizations. In their place the performer's life is complicated by less familiar ways of using the piano as both a stringed and percussion instrument, and as an instrument invested with interesting properties of resonance.

Tape and Double demands from the performer a rather broad range of unorthodox techniques culled from practices found as early as Schoenberg's *Three Piano Pieces* of 1909, the sympathetic vibration of strings, to the already mentioned double attack of Krenek's own invention. Also in evidence are resonant body blows and timbral preparations of the piano strings as introduced by John Cage, certain Ives and Cowell-derived hand and forearm clusters, as well as a varied assortment of "inside piano" percussion and string effects. Krenek asks the pianist to "hit central strings inside with light felt mallet," to glissando across the strings, to produce a vertical glissando by pinching "one of the lightly overspun strings sharply with two fingers and rub it vigorously toward the keyboard."

The purpose of these special techniques becomes quite clear on hearing *Tape and Double*. Krenek was, obviously, very much aware of interesting similarities of piano and electronic timbres while composing this piece. What resulted is a strikingly lively and, in some moments, humorous virtuoso piano work that, given adequate tape playback equipment, should delight audiences of two-piano teams just about anywhere.

III

At some point in the 1940s Krenek seemed to suffer from an embarrassment of riches to the extent that he stopped numbering his work before reaching opus 100. He now seems to have resigned himself to the ignominy of fecundity for *Tape and Double* carries an opus number, 207. Since that was in 1970 and since Krenek's seventieth birthday in August of that year multiplied the demands on the composer for new works, including an opera commissioned by the Hamburg opera, it is apparent that his waterline continues to lap floodstage for which we can all be grateful.

For surely Krenek will be recognized as one of the masters of the twentieth century and, above all others, the composer who continued to maintain the most vigorous interest in all performance media. His output is too vast for any of us to know comprehensively at this time, but it is apparent that Krenek has spoken in meaningful terms for five decades of the twentieth century and that he continues to make definitive contributions to contemporary currents of musical thought. Should we desire to take a seismographic reading of the eruptive artistic movements of our time, we would do well to search out the contributions of Ernst Krenek.

Those of us in at least occasional contact with his vast output will have their own favorites based on personal experience. Mine relate to the years surrounding my own studies with Krenek in Minnesota: the *Cantata for War Time* (1944) for mezzo soprano, women's chorus, and orchestra based on poems of Herman Melville; the magnificent *Lamentatio Jeremiae Prophetae,* a portion of which we students heard in the middle forties owing to the efforts of the brilliant college choral conductor, Robert Holliday; the attractive *Seventh String Quartet* of 1943–44 as performed by Rudolph Kolisch and his Pro Arte Quartet based at the University of Wisconsin; the powerful *Symphonic Elegy;* the charming *Five Players* for women's chorus on the Litany of John Donne; the excellent *Sonata for Violin and Piano* of 1944–45 as played by the American violinist Louis Krasner.

But there are both later and earlier treasures to be discovered, among the former a delightful set of *Five Pieces for Trombone and Piano* commissioned by the trombone virtuoso Stuart Dempster, or Krenek's setting of six Karl Barth poems for soprano and piano, *Wechselrahmen,* of 1965. I am especially fond of the lesser known sequel to Krenek's *Sestina* (known through its recording with soprano Bethany Beardsley) called *Quintina,* which sets

Krenek's own poem on the musical process for soprano, flute, viola, electric guitar, percussion, and tape.

The immediacy and felicity of Krenek's music comes as a surprise to those who have heard of Krenek the constructivist or Krenek the esoteric musico-mathematician. Within the huge Krenek repertory, there are both more and less accessible pieces, works more monumental and serious, and music that converses easily with us and even entertains us. Among the latter is Krenek's recent *Duo* for flute and contrabass, with prerecorded flute and bass, written for Nancy and Bertram Turetzky. As example of the former, I would like to speak briefly of Krenek's profoundly felt tribute to Anton Webern, *Instant Remembered* (1967–68), a multi-languaged cycle for soprano, narrator, and a large instrumental ensemble, along with a prerecorded string quartet.

I would expect a new listener to *Instant Remembered* to be most aware of its changing web of instrumental timbres: the thin, hard-edged texture formed from its majority of single entering sounds and its reliance on one-, two-, and three-tone motives. The listener will also be aware of an expressive vocal line, primarily syllabic and speech rhythmed. And, although the variation from song to song is lyrically dramatic, he will realize *Instant Remembered* to be an expertly controlled structure of satisfying proportions.

The point to be made is that we have much to learn from a composer of Krenek's stature, from a composer who has been consistently a man of his time. But it is obvious that we must have more opportunities to experience Krenek's music if we are to take advantage of his power of insight and creative projection. The signs of the times point to a rapidly improving situation in this regard. This allows us to hope that the full significance of Krenek's work will be recognized in America as well as in Europe as Stravinsky prophesied in 1960: "But Krenek will be honored one day even at home."

IV

The origin of the series of essays that follow this introduction to Krenek and his music begins to bear out Stravinsky's prophesy of 1960. These essays were requested as public lectures by the University of California at San Diego to help celebrate Krenek's seventieth year, and as a means of stimulating him to take a retrospective look at the times and fortunes of one contemporary musican who had so decisively helped shape the artistic character of his century. Krenek presented the four lectures, one a week, before an intimate audience of students, faculty, and townsfolk, while in residence as a Regent's Lecturer on the San Diego campus in January and February of 1970.

This was not Krenek's first association with the San Diego campus, far from it. In 1966 Krenek had lectured there on the sketchbooks of Anton Webern and during that particular visit his *Quintina* was performed. Later, on the occasion of the inauguration of the university's John Muir College, Krenek was honored as one of five founding fellows of the college.

On the evening of that event, these honored fellows and invited guests of the university heard Krenek's new orchestral piece, *Exercises of a Late Hour,* a work commissioned by a friend of John Muir College and twice conducted that evening by the composer. Two years later when the permanent campus of John Muir College was dedicated (its buildings having sprung from the coastal desert like dragon's teeth, or so it seemed), a large assemblage of students, faculty, and friends listened to the first West Coast performance of *Instant Remembered,* which was repeated for the Los Angeles Monday Evening Concerts nine days later. It was during that particular academic celebration that Krenek presented the four lectures now offered in this book, as a series of four essays on the historical, political, sociological-economic, and technical background of one contemporary musician and composer.

Not only is Krenek known as a respected composer and theorist but also, as a keen observer and an articulate, critical writer. He is familiar with several languages and is intimately conversant with a broad range of music literature. Although Krenek's native tongue is German, he handles the English language with precision and wit. Of course, public lectures prepared for students and laymen apply broader brushstrokes than do more technical writings. That Krenek tackled his assignment with the same candid care he would have expended on a closely reasoned and analytical lecture tells us much about the man and his essential dedication as a musician and teacher.

One could well observe that Ernst Krenek is always the same, seemingly a model of intellectual and emotional consistency. He appears to wear only one hat and to show a single face to all and sundry. But it is well known that as a young and radical Viennese composer Krenek still found the time to read through operettas of Jacques Offenbach. Later, American colleagues have reported Krenek's evident pleasure in playing four-hand Mozart and Schubert. But one must also take note that the same composer-pianist performed Alban Berg's gnarly Concerto for violin, piano and wind instruments; that he has conducted the difficult music of his contemporaries, as well as his own; and that he writes his own opera librettos, whether satirical comedy or monumental tragedy, either in English or in German.

It would not be too surprising to find that Krenek is better known to some as a writer of words given the relative rarity of new music performances and the easy currency of books. Two book-length writings of Krenek are at present available in English. One is a compilation of essays and articles titled *Exploring Music*, which spans twenty-seven years from 1929 to 1956. The other is the well read and influential *Music Here And Now*, first published in English in 1939 and recently reissued by a different publisher.

Exploring Music includes writings of a rather broad range of musical subjects, some essays written while Krenek was attached to a German newspaper, others as occasional articles for various journals. They are all richly informative and yet unpretentious. One of my favorites is Krenek's account of how, in Stuttgart, he came to write music for a puppet play. Actually, the essay reveals Krenek's fascination with puppets. He tells us how they are put together, how they are operated, and how one goes about producing a puppet play when no one knows anything. This delightful feuilleton seems today like a mirror held up to the essential, unchanging personality of its author. It reveals his inherent curiosity, his essential liveliness, his energy, and his modest good humor.

And so, I believe, do the following essays. Without pontificating or belaboring, Krenek reveals his own earnest philosophical commitments to living and art. He does so in a modest and, yet, not unattached manner that allows him to admit less than full success with this or that enterprise, even when the undertaking was his desire to continue the great symphonic tradition after Mahler. In these essays Krenek again unconsciously holds up the mirror to the man as much as to the composer and musician of the twentieth century.

V

Krenek's four University of California lectures were conceived as a whole from what their author determined to be four basic vectors bisecting the contemporary composer's metier and existence: historical, political, socioeconomic, and technical influences on, and aspects of, his craft and living. These are not, then, a mere collection of individual essays but a comprehensive and integrated overview seen along the angles of Krenek's consideration. Along the way Krenek illumines fundamental tenets of his own positioning as he tries to see past and present through, as he says, the windows of his own personality. But from the beginning Krenek admits to a wariness of what he believes to be the futile preoccupation of historians: their questing after objective, historical truth.

Krenek doubts that historical objectivity can be anything more than an illusion. Events are too transient and their reporting too subjective. There are too many viewpoints, including the prejudice of the historian himself. This skeptical attitude seems to have matured in part during Krenek's struggles with writing the complex drama for his monumental opera, *Karl V*, which probes for the reasons why the emperor of half the world should have abdicated his power and responsibility.

A second insight expressed in the opening essay seems as provocative as this admitted skepticism of historical truth. Krenek seems to hold the opinion that artistic inevitability is not willed, or accomplished merely because it has been striven for, but that it results, seemingly, in spite of personal intent, purposes, and efforts. In forming that insight Krenek was looking back on his own personal artistic *angst* over the historical crisis in idiom and expression which was the lot of his particular generation.

Arnold Schoenberg had become Krenek's bête noire in those days, as he must have been for an entire generation of composers seeking a closer contact with the here and now, with the optimism of a reconstructing Europe. Its young artists wanted to define a more positive reaffirmation of living, although without any trace of romantic idealism or innocence. They found Schoenberg's complex atonal idiom, derived from an expressionist ethos as much as from a fundamental transformation of the tonal language, irritatingly in the way—an obstacle that refused to move, a presence that refused to disappear.

In the 1920s Krenek was regarded as a leader of this youthful generation and he, like many of his colleagues, could not stomach what seemed at the time the overheated emotional atmosphere of the Schoenberg school. Moreover, neither did the fashionable German neoclassicism appeal to the young Austrian—it was found too academic and humorless. No wonder Krenek was intrigued by the more flippant neoclassicism of Paris. As Krenek reminds us, Parisian-style neoclassicism only used the past for its own sophisticated masquerades instead of taking it seriously. Parisian surrealism struck a responsive chord in the young Austrian from 1925 through 1929, at a time when the composer had exhausted his earlier atonal radicalism, or at least tired of its aggressive behavior. But Krenek had gone to Berlin to complete his studies with Franz Schreker and there the pianist Eduard Erdmann inflamed Krenek to turn back toward the model of Schubert's early romanticism. Somehow this seemed compatible with Krenek's infatuation with Paris. Yet in the Schubertian model resided an essential universal classicism posed by Beethoven. This was bound to present Krenek with a contradiction to his polemic opposition to the Schoenberg school, since Schoenberg was actually the contemporary carrier of that tradition.

So Schubert became the catalyst that opened Krenek's eyes to the structural classicism of Schoenberg's music, now grammatically organized by means of Schoenberg's method of composing with tone rows. Krenek does not claim a direct line of development from Schubert to Schoenberg but the lineage seems implicit as one reads these essays and Krenek's earlier accounting in *Music Here And Now.* The historical truth seems to be that Krenek did finally arrive in Schoenberg country, perhaps in spite of himself and, certainly, after publicly opposing the language and manner of

Schoenberg. Only after the dust settled could Krenek look back and see the inevitability of that arrival point.

Krenek cites as a second example of his belief in extra-conscious, historical inevitability the transformation of his own rotational method of maneuvering note segments, developed in the early 1940s, into the kind of serialism he initiated in the 1950s. He himself became aware of the technical connection a decade after the fait accompli. He had not planned the application of this rotational technique to the structuring of musical parameters other than pitch nor was he fully conscious of doing so until some time after the fact. Krenek has expanded to changes in technique the intuitive relating that Schoenberg and others discovered within the thematics of some given composition.

There is even Krenek the musicologist: a monograph on Johannes Ockeghem, the carefully studied *caput* masses of the fifteenth century and, in general, a firsthand familiarity with a broad range of music literature. Discovering the intricate motivic workings of Gregorian chant and the cantus firmus techniques of early polyphonic composers must have been reassuring to Krenek the composer, as he developed his own methods of using the row and his own compositional principles.

Krenek credits the excellent music library at Vassar for his renewed interest in music history. There he browsed and then earnestly studied early music documents, in spite of the evident disapproval of his musicologist "boss." When Krenek moved on to Hamline, his interest in historical studies fired up, he found an impoverished research library in comparison with the one he had enjoyed at Vassar. Only the new availability of microfilm and a handful of bright, energetic graduate students encouraged him to pursue those studies, which resulted in the two-volume publication, *Hamline Studies in Musicology*.

Krenek reveals in these essays his unflagging fascination with ideas whether historical, political, or philosophical. He admits to concern with extramusical ideas as a composer but only as a composer of opera. He makes it very clear that he thinks music alone conveys no extra musical implications. "Music is completely neutral . . . its movement can only be understood as an image of the intensity of emotion but never as a likeness of its object."

Twice in recent operas Krenek has arranged for a confrontation between the historical or mythological past and the present. The most recent occasion was in his opera *Der goldene Bock* based loosely on the story of the golden fleece. The opera's characters travel back and forth through time as well as space as they search for their security blanket. In an opera written for Bavarian television, *Der Zauberspiegel,* Krenek allows, through the grace of technology, an Italian painter of Marco Polo's time to step out of a painting into the modern world and just as mercifully to step back into the painting when the experience becomes too disagreeable.

Krenek's abiding concern in his operas is with the implications of freedom. This was the concern of his earliest opera, *Zwingburg.* Later, Krenek suggested the possibility of opting out entirely in his one act opera, *Das geheime Königreich,* and, conversely, has Charles attempt to answer God's query as to whether or not his abdication from responsibility was justified.

The opposite side of the coin for Krenek is responsibility and somehow the two must get along together. Krenek has examined the repression of freedom and dictatorial authority also. In the second of the following essays Krenek reveals that he intended to dedicate his opera *Pallas Athena weint,* an elaboration of the story of Socrates in terms of our modern predicament and with an eye on the American present, to Adlai Stevenson. He points out at the same time that he had developed the character of Mélethos with the image of Senator Joseph McCarthy in mind. Not that Krenek thinks a composer can influence the real world as a composer. Not by a jot. He advises letters to the editor and other real-world activities to attain such ends. But he knows that the politics of the real world can exert strong influences on the composer. The story he tells of political harassment, forcing cancellation of the production of *Karl V*, has been repeated in the experience of other composers during and after the period of Hitler's coming to power. And, in this essay, Krenek relates the activist career of Richard Wagner with a preciseness of detail that suggests keen interest.

But then Krenek has always seemed an unlimited storehouse of knowledge. It is just this casual but detailed awareness of so many subjects in and around music that astounds. One might expect a composer to have a firm handle on the subject of musical style or on the history of music theory. We might even expect him to be able to write a motet in Palestrina style or complete a Schubert piano sonata. But who would really expect such a composer to also have a compendious knowledge of the social status or economic condition of composers from the Middle Ages to the present, including a very clear and articulate understanding of how copyright laws and performance rights societies work? I know of few sources as informationally useful on these subjects as Krenek's third essay.

But then, Krenek admits to a very compelling motivation when discussing in his fourth essay on compositional technique, why he decided to explore the possibilities of serialism. "I am glad to admit that it was just curiosity which I think is a very legitimate motivation for any kind of artistic progress." Who would doubt that Krenek would think the same motivation invalid in the realm of knowledge and who would doubt that curiosity, at least in part, accounts for Krenek's encyclopedic awareness of the composer's everyday world, as well as of his artistic world and its ideas?

Circling My Horizon

by ERNST KRENEK

I

On these pages I propose to sketch a panorama of our musical situation as observed through the windows of my personality and delineated by the positions that were assigned to me in the changing scenes. Obviously, the picture will be subjective, which I hope shall not impair its relative validity, especially since I will try to show that objectivity is intrinsically impossible and, when it is attempted, illusionary. If I thus limit the perspectives of my design to my own field of vision, I hope that this will not be interpreted as an expression of egotism or vanity. Much as I have from time to time desired to occupy the vantage point of a detached observer who would faithfully register the sum total of the phenomena offered to his view, it was my fate to become always actively involved in the process that would come under the consideration of comprehensive criticism. Thus my ruminations are inevitably conditioned by the changing positions of creative personality. It would seem to me insincere if I should pretend that I am able to disregard these limitations, and therefore I have to accept them for better or worse.

My presentation is articulated in four sections. The first is concerned with the position in history of the contemporary composer and with the varying degrees of his historical consciousness and the ways in which his work is influenced by these factors. In the second I discuss the composer's involvement in the problems of the society of which he is a member. This subject matter I have mainly illustrated by referring to my operas, of which I have written twenty, since a good number of these works have very outspoken political implications. In the third section I talk about the sociological and economic background of the composer's work as it has unfolded in our century. To conclude this series of informal communications, I focus on the particular situation of composition at the present time, discussing the concept of serialism, and investigating how it developed and what became of it.

Let us consider first the nature of history. If we define history as the sum total of things past, we have to realize that it exists only to the extent of our knowledge of it. We may experience the consequences of something that has happened in the past, but this in itself does not suffice to make us know that it happened. And unless we know this, the particular event might just as well never have happened. The nearly unique source of "our historical knowledge" is the report that was made by some witness of the event and was left for us to peruse. The historian's resolution to give faithful account of what happened exactly as it happened—or as it has become fashionable to say, "to tell it like it is"—is an illusion that must remain wishful thinking to a high degree, for he depends on reports that were drawn up by human beings who were biased in hundreds of different ways. And the historian, sifting those reports, is himself prejudiced even if he should not be aware of it, his prejudice being generated by the sequence of the very events he is planning to explicate. Insight of this kind became available to me only when I immersed myself into the mysteries of history preparing my opera *Karl V,* about which I shall have more to say later.

At the beginning of my career as a composer, around 1920, when I had reached the same age as our century, my historical consciousness was at a very elementary level. In the composition classes of my teacher, Frank Schreker, in Vienna, we heard very little about music history. He did not think very highly of the musicological studies that went on at the university and the conservatory. The teaching of history was greatly limited to abstract descriptions of styles and endless lists of composers' names whose music we never heard nor saw. For at that time there were no records or tapes to listen to and no microfilms of ancient music to look at. Thus the composition students knew hardly any music before Bach. We studied sixteenth-century interpretation by Johann Joseph Fux of the idiom of Palestrina, whose music we never touched.

The purpose of this training was to endow the students with a sense of discipline and to make them aware of the importance of technique, meaning that they should understand that one cannot rely on inspiration alone but must also have enough skill to keep going on the assumptions of a certain stylistic image. The acquisition of such know-how was supposed to be indispensable when we were turned loose as "free" composers. While in the regimented field of strict counterpoint every note was scrutinized for its correctness according to the rules, in free composition we were left more or less to our own devices. Criticism was vague, perfunctory, and capricious. The general idea was that the music to be written by the young composers should sound good and be original, which was interpreted to mean mainly that it should not be obvious or commonplace, and "modern," that is, fitting into the generally accepted concept of progress, but not shocking or absurd.

The concept of progress, of course, implied some sort of historical consciousness. It is based on the assumption that the events of history follow one another as a chain of causes and effects wherein the causes are observed, ascertained, and analyzed by man so that he may control and bring about the effects in such a way that the subsequent state of affairs will be better than the previous one, whatever he may set up as the ultimate ideal goal of this wonderful process.

In terms of the musical situation in which I found myself, as I described it before, progress meant that the musical idiom of Wagner was better than that of Haydn or Beethoven, because he dared to use more dissonant chords and delay their resolutions more ingeniously; that songs by Hugo Wolf were better than those by Franz Schubert for similar reasons, which made them more communicative for the modern mind, and so forth. From all this it followed that we were trained to go on in the same spirit, discover new dissonances, and disguise the facts of tonality more cleverly. Thus we moved about in a territory vaguely delineated by the landmarks set up by Debussy, Max Reger, Richard Strauss, and perhaps Scriabin. This was the generally accepted image of modernism. Franz Schreker, who was at home in that territory, was considered pretty progressive, while Schoenberg was looked upon as a dangerous lunatic.

In fact, the difference between the more moderate conventions in which I launched my first compositional ventures and the seemingly radical philosophy of the Schoenberg circle was more one of degree than of essence. Schoenberg too was a believer in progressive moving along a one-way street toward higher and more valuable achievements. He had, however, an infinitely keener intellect than Schreker, was much more articulate and more courageous in living up to the conclusions he had derived from his view of history. But at the time I am speaking of, in the first quarter of the century, he was either praised as a revolutionary prophet who cleared away the useless rubble of the past or damned as a subversive nihilist bent upon tearing down venerable conventions established by a glorious past. When my teacher was called to Berlin around 1921 to become director of the Academy of Music, I followed him, ostensibly to complete my formal studies in music. Actually, I received the academy's diploma, which made me a sort of licensed composer, whatever that may mean, more or less on sufferance, for I had drifted away from the official line of thinking long before. More than ever I was convinced that the young composer had to serve the cause of progress. But, now, to be progressive meant to break away from the traditional concepts with much more daring and conviction. As much as I knew of Schoenberg's music, which was little or nothing, to me it still remained rather obscure. I was more attracted by the elemental features of Béla Batók and began to write music that dispensed rather cavalierly with the respectability of tonal relationships and was rich in dissonant polyphony and rhythmic insistence on protracted ostinatos.

At that time I produced quantities of music at a speed that today is quite incomprehensible to me. I am unable to figure out how it was possible even mechanically to write down so many notes in so short a time, not to mention the creative effort that had to go with it or before it. In addition to the sheer number of compositions, many of them were rather bulky long works. Today I do not see a contradiction here, for it seems to me that the habit of writing fast promotes the production of long, possibly repetitious and loquacious pieces, while a propensity for writing slowly induces concentration and economy.

My main interest was devoted to the form of the symphony, and in this I can see a certain symptom of being conscious of historical continuity. I remember distinctly, for I even put it down as a note in a diary I used to keep off and on, that I had decided to try to become the successor of Mahler in the field of the symphony. First I wrote no less than three symphonies at the age of twenty-three and each one of them has, in my opinion, retained to this day some elements of vitality. The fact that I did not approach the problem of the symphony for another twenty years should, however, indicate that I was not quite convinced of the validity of the project. When I took it up again in the 1940s, I found the results rather disappointing. My only comfort is that nobody else has succeeded any better in continuing the great symphonic tradition.

A considerable number of my modernistic compositions originated in those years of the early twenties. In looking back at them, I notice that their generally atonal idiom here and there includes isolated fragments of the language of tradition, usually evoking memories of a very early stage of the musical materials not yet touched by the late romantic mannerism of chromatics. Such encapsulated remnants of another age evoke frequently a feeling of nostalgia and melancholy. The procedure as such is related to the principles of surrealism, of which at that time I had not the slightest idea.

Elements of surrealism also characterize the movement of neoclassicism. It began to be noticeable at that time and was to become the dominant musical style for more than two decades. In terms of the notion of history as a one-way street leading onward and upward, neoclassicism evidently was an antiprogressive, contrary movement in that it professed the wish to restore ancient manners of musical design. At the same time it looked progressive, for it was designed to do away with the romanticism of the preceding generation, of which Schoenberg's expressionism seemed to be an obsolete continuation.

As I remember it, the first manifestation of this trend

was Stravinsky's *Pulcinella*, in which he transcribed, rewrote and remodeled materials fished out from the work of the early eighteenth-century Italian composer, Pergolesi. This set the tone for most of the retrospective efforts to come. The late seventeenth and eighteenth centuries were the primary targets of the restorative activities of neoclassicism. Of course, the reactionary aspects of this movement made it highly popular with a public frightened by the progressive attitude of the Schoenberg school, by what was called the destructive excesses of expressionism. The situation was not really as simple as all that, because the neoclassicists, especially Stravinsky, did not just excavate the old models to imitate them in their new creations. They treated them rather as pleasing and attractive relics of a better age. They presented the models with all the damage and scars inflicted upon them by time. Today by hindsight we are able to state that in this respect neoclassicism was progressive after all, for the concept of fragmentation, of the broken-up whole, of the irrevocable alienation of its parts, was to survive and succeed the age of neoclassicism. But at the time one could not know this. And actually the victory of these progressive, albeit negative aspects of neoclassicism was based on entirely different premises, as we shall see.

Another element that made neoclassicism interesting, even for the followers of the atonal expressionistic tendencies, was the emphasis on objectivity. The public, repelled by the sharp dissonances of the atonal idiom, did not recognize that these dissonances were the inevitable result of carrying further, and on to the bitter end, the essential features of the beloved late romanticism: the emotional exuberance that had made Wagner, Strauss, and related composers so dear to audiences wallowing in soulfulness, as long as it was contained within the boundaries of an ever-so-expanded tonality, had eventually exploded beyond these lines and brought about the wild gestures, violent contrasts, cutting dissonances, and improbable melodic jumps of the expressionistic idiom. Some of the younger adepts, myself among them, became a little tired of the overheated emotionalism of the style and began to dream of the cool, detached, objective music that would rely on perfect construction rather than on exuding sentiment.

The concept of the autonomy of music as a law unto itself began to take powerful root. For composers who embraced this concept, neoclassicism seemed to carry a significant message, even if they would not agree with its reactionary program. Personally, I have not conscientiously or consistently followed the line of neoclassicism. In Germany, under the influence of sociological considerations that I shall discuss later, neoclassicism took on a distinctly restorative shape when composers such as Hindemith started to revive the concerto grosso style of the late seventeenth and early eighteenth century. The busy contrapuntal texture of Bach became the chief model of these compositional endeavors. To my taste the results often were academic, betraying too obviously the historical consciousness of the authors, and pedantic in displaying fatiguing sameness of color and texture.

During this period strenuous efforts were made everywhere to create national musical styles. Composers were assiduously delving into the materials provided by folkloristic research. Nearly all this work was neoclassically oriented, be it only because the raw material was easily adaptable to traditional treatment. Bartók was about the only composer who tried in his most important works to interpret the folklore stuff in different ways. It is remarkable that these nationalistic tendencies, for decades so vociferously advanced, petered out totally after the Second World War, and fortunately so.

I was eventually more attracted by the French variety of neoclassicism as represented by Stravinsky, Milhaud,

Honegger, and others. The occasional touches of surrealistic irony lend some of the works a flavor of charming roguishness. The ancient model, slightly damaged by a few wrong notes in the harmony, by rhythmic distortions, by anachronistic instrumental color, is quoted in a surprising context rather than reconstructed with resources brought up to date. Another aspect that made this newly discovered province of music highly interesting was the introduction of jazz elements. At that time in central Europe, very little was known about American jazz, which began to penetrate the Continent only after the conclusion of the First World War. The little we knew about it corresponded very well with our wishes for a clean, crisp, clear-cut, unsentimental, objective music. Nearly all European composers of that time reacted to the new phenomenon by incorporating some of its characteristics into their so-called serious music. As far as I know, only the members of the Schoenberg school never gave in to the temptation. They were too thoroughly steeped in the idea of incompatibility of serious and entertainment music, which had been regarded for nearly a hundred years as an unshakable axiom.

My own private turnabout from modernism became, eventually, somewhat different from everybody else's reactionary spree, of which I probably could be proud if I cared to. I did not visualize returning to the seventeenth century but to the early romanticism of Franz Schubert. On the surface this can probably be well enough explained as owing to personal circumstances. When I arrived in Berlin as a student, I struck up close friendship with a pianist and composer, Eduard Erdmann, a few years my senior. He happened to be an enthusiastic devotee of Schubert's music and, since he had the temperament of a forceful evangelist and I was at a highly impressionable age, I was easily swayed to share his admiration for the Viennese master. More elaborate explanations would probably take into account that my hailing from the same Vienna may have caused a sort of selective affinity when, under the influence of the general tendency to look backward, I searched for a model at the time of my rising doubts about the validity of my own atonal exploits. Historical research might hit upon still other motivations. I am using this very small marginal detail of my private *curriculum vitae* to illustrate what I mentioned about the relativity of historical material.

My neoromantic period lasted about five years. The main product of my occasional preoccupation with jazz is the opera *Jonny spielt auf,* which became so successful and famous that it even infiltrated the Metropolitan Opera House in New York forty years ago. It created a tremendous sensation for reasons that I found entirely wrong, a fact that irritated me a great deal. It was labeled a "jazz opera," which I felt to be a misnomer, for whatever jazz there occurs is brought in to characterize the professional sphere of the protagonist, Jonny, leader of an American combo. The music attached to the other characters, which to me were at least as important, is conceived in that early romantic idiom I had chosen as my model, occasionally touched up with dissonant spices and Italianizing Pucciniesque vocal exuberance. The label of "jazz opera" could, if at all, be affixed much rather to a later work that I wrote in this period, *Leben des Orest.* Here the jazzy flavor permeates one clearly defined sector of the stage action, to create a sort of colloquial musical language, a musical *linqua franca* of our time. In later years it has been held against these pieces that the jazz displayed in them was really no jazz at all, or at best a very poor, primitive specimen. This is true enough and hardly worth pointing out. What I brought into play was not a replica of the real thing, which I might not even have done if I had known the real thing. But I tried to project the reflections of the image of jazz which I had formed in my mind on the basis of my very scanty knowledge of it, just as I projected in this opera an idealistic wish-dream of America, in the vein of similar pictures drawn by the early romanticists. Of the real America I know hardly more than that it was the land of gangsters and prohibition, and neither aspect was inviting.

For my ostensibly reactionary exploits, I also fabricated a little theory to the effect that the newly discovered means of musical expression, that is, the atonal vocabulary, should not prevent the use of the old ones, and that it should be possible to restore the old vocabulary to its original power and freshness, through something vaguely mystical which I called *Urerlebnis*, or primordial experience. In this I hoped to differentiate myself constructively from my fellow modernists of the Schoenberg school who promoted the idea that the new idiom had superseded the old and rendered the meaningful use of the old resources impossible. Only Alban Berg was striving for a synthesis in accordance with his conciliatory, warmhearted temperament, but he arrived at different results. I do not know how successful the application of my *Urerlebnis* has been. Some of the works that originated in this frame of mind, especially groups and cycles of songs, have retained a great deal of vitality. Nonetheless, I noticed that after a while I had run out of steam on this track and that it was time to look for a promising switch if I intended to keep going at all.

The alternatives were giving up composing entirely or at least for an indefinite period, and returning to modernism. While I considered the former seriously and concentrated for some time on literary work, the latter won out and I began a somewhat gingerly approach to the twelve-tone technique, which in the meantime had been developed by Schoenberg. Today when the highbrow musical magazines abound with analyses and detailed descriptions of compositional procedure, it is hardly believable that for years the only source of information on the twelve-tone technique was a rather vague and not entirely accurate essay in a Vienna periodical. The practitioners of the technique whom I knew, Alban Berg and Anton Webern, were quite reticent about what they were doing and it seemed indelicate to become too inquisitive. Thus, I had to rely on my own research which was slow and laborious, although the basic principles of this technique were simple enough. But it was a completely new and unaccustomed way of musical thinking.

Among musicians at large and laymen as well, the twelve-tone technique was regarded as an aggravated case of atonality or, worse, as the desperate effort of a composer who had run out of inspiration. During my romantic excursion I had shared this view and even incurred Schoenberg's wrath by putting a few sarcastic remarks into a lecture of mine. The traces of the master's anguish may be found in the preface of his *Satires* for chorus, where he deposited a not too brilliant pun upon my name. Later I apologized for the immature dig and we lived in peace ever after.

It is easy nowadays to interpret the inauguration of the twelve-tone technique historically as a part of the general tendency of restoration prevailing during the 1920s. At that time it appeared to be a radically new departure, and the dialectical truth probably is that it was both. This technique may now be seen as a conservative factor because it imposed a strict discipline onto the chaotic world of atonality. The rationalization, leaking out from the inner circle, was that the atonal composers had realized that without some kind of constructive order only short pieces of music could be written and that the revived desire of creating larger forms prompted the invention of a new discipline. Another explanation was that in order to secure the atonal character of the idiom, it was necessary to prevent any tone from gaining, through repetition, too much weight and becoming a tonal center in the old sense. To achieve this end, it became desirable to systematize the order of succession of our twelve-pitch classes before entering the actual process of composition, so that none could reappear before the other eleven had been sounded. Be that as it may, a trend toward the restoration of law and order certainly promoted the invention of the twelve-tone technique. This conjecture is corroborated by the fact that a substantial number of Schoenberg's dodecaphonic works are structured after the pattern of the classical sonata form. They are different from the exercises of neoclassicism in that the twelve-tone school tried to revive the spirit of the old forms, while neoclassicism presented replicas of their facades with interesting cracks added.

Historical perspective reveals that the advent of atonality was experienced by the public as a violent shock, while the introduction of the twelve-tone method caused hardly a ripple—just slightly raised eyebrows among tradition-minded experts, although it would have been logical had it happened the other way around. For atonality had been foreshadowed, as the evolutionists would say, ever since Wagner's generation had pushed toward the limits of tonality, while the idea of preorganizing the musical material according to abstract serial patterns was something radically new. It did not register that way because the character of the musical idiom, the sound material that was perceived, remained roughly the same regardless of whether it was ordered serially or freely piled up in atonal clusters. Conversely, the earlier transition from harmonies ever so loosely strung together in a tonal net to those seemingly unrelated dissonant clusters was shockingly conspicuous.

My own first venture in the new technique was a most ambitious one. It was the full-length historical opera *Karl V*. I shall discuss later its extramusical implications which will make clear that I considered the project one of utmost importance in every respect. This attitude prompted me to make it also the point of departure for a completely new stage of my musical development. After this opera I wrote two works, a set of variations for piano and my Sixth String Quartet, in which I perhaps explored most thoroughly the truly progressive aspects of the twelve-tone technique; at least I see it today in this light. Later, after 1937, when I had come to live in America, I oriented myself more toward Schoenberg's inclination for reviving the sonata form. It would be easy to say that this happened under the influence of the conformist American atmosphere or perhaps was prompted by the hope of my becoming somewhat more acceptable to a musical community told by the critical experts that the twelve-tone technique was a freakish conceit of a small Viennese group of neurotics, and that American music happily had left such aberrations far behind. When in the 1940s I experimented with relaxing the structures of the old twelve-tone technique by introducing a new concept that I called "rotation," it may have appeared to be a dubious attempt at compromise. In fact, however, this does not seem to have been the true motivation, because the first work in which I applied the rotational technique, my *Lamentatio Jeremiae Prophetae,* turned out to be fiendishly difficult, so that it had to wait for sixteen years before it was produced in its entirety. About as many years later I realized that my rotational technique was my first tentative step into the still undiscovered territory of serialism, for by the term rotation I wanted to describe progressive switching of the tones within the twelve-tone series according to premeditated patterns, in order to obtain additional derivative forms of the basic set.

It was only in America that I became fully conscious and cognizant of music history, but as it again seems, purely by chance. It so happened that the place of my first teaching assignment, Vassar College, had a magnificent music library in which I loved to browse. Obviously I was ready for this new experience, for I was under no obligation to use that library. As a matter of fact, my boss, a hidebound musicologist, did not like it at all. Soon enough I stopped browsing and began to study more and more seriously. Probably subconsciously, I looked for prototypes of our own compositional procedures and eventually I found astonishing parallels. My attention was especially attracted by the design of Gregorian chant and by the complexities of fifteenth-century polyphony. To my dismay I noticed that the majority of musicologists whose work I greatly admired and appreciated because it had provided me with otherwise inaccessible material for historical study—that these scholars almost resented a composer's interest in their work and I regretted that they did not reciprocate this interest at all. The tension thus created led to the termination of my tenure at Vassar College, and I became head of the music department at Hamline University in St. Paul, Minnesota. Only then could I continue my historical studies undisturbed, for I was my own boss. There was only one slight drawback: I had practically no library. When this obstacle was to some degree overcome through the extensive use of microfilms, I was able with the aid of a group of outstanding graduate students to achieve some results that gave us, at least, if nobody else, a great deal of satisfaction. My own particular object of study was the music of Johannes Ockeghem, which I find fascinating to this day.

I have been criticized because I apparently found it necessary to search for historical prototypes in order to justify modern compositional methods. I feel that such objections are based on a misunderstanding. The fact that the melismata of Gregorian chant displayed inversion and retrogression, or the fact that some medieval composers like Dufay used the cantus firmi as basic melodic patterns from which they derived individual motivic shapes for their polyphonic designs, did not in my opinion justify application of such procedures in the twelve-tone technique. Obviously, the only justification of any technique is the accomplishment of viable results. What I was interested in was observing and experiencing the permanency of certain ways of musical thinking. I was also interested in the existence of archetypes that seemed to run through the known history of occidental music and, from time to time, to crystallize in the shape of stylistic entities. In my teaching I asked the students to undergo thorough training in sixteenth-century counterpoint, the rules of which were derived as far as possible from the practice of the old masters directly, not because I wanted them to revive the style of Palestrina but in order to make them aware of the function of strict technical discipline in relation to a body of totally controlled live music, so that they would be able to apply this experience to their excursions into new, so far unknown, and not yet controlled territory.

Today I am no longer so convinced that this historical orientation is as necessary or useful as I thought under the impact of my own historical study. The nineteenth century entertained the enviably naïve notion that all that had happened before was either welcome preparation of its own ultimate excellence, or deplorable detour and delay. I remember having seen an edition, published about 1890, of a work by Dufay, in which the commentator criticized the fifteenth-century composer for not yet knowing how to modulate properly from D-minor to C-sharp. It did not occur to him that Dufay never thought of modulating anywhere but worked on entirely different assumptions. But in the eyes of the modern critic, it was just that which made his music appear inferior. It may be true that strong ages are not lost in awe and admiration of history because they are too occupied with creating and building their own things. The Baroque era was one of those periods. The artists of that time had no qualms about tearing down or disfiguring the most venerable monuments of the Gothic because they found them obsolete and unsightly and were convinced that they had something far superior to substitute for the ancient stuff. It is fortunate that to assert itself in music, a new generation does not need to destroy the works of its ancestors. It is sufficient to let them gather dust on the shelves of the library.

Whether ignorance or even contempt of history reveals strength or weakness or just laziness and self-indulgence can be ascertained only by evaluating the products of such mentality. But this evaluation is in turn a function of historical processes. If we feel that history takes its course according to some inexorable internal necessity, it would not seem to make very much difference whether or not we are aware of its preordained pattern. If we feel that we are *making* history as free agents, we may not pay much attention to precedent, only to be told afterward that our actions were a logical consequence of all that went before. "To be or not to be historically oriented" is a question that cannot be answered any better than the question "To be or not to be," period—or rather, question mark.

II

To be or not to be politically engaged is a question that has been put to a composer—or that he would ask his own conscience—only fairly recently. Before the nineteenth century a question of this kind seemed to be entirely irrelevant. We can not imagine that Palestrina or Bach had any pronounced political views or, if they did, how they would have expressed them. In Mozart's work we think we can discover traces of political consciousness; his choice of Beaumarchais's *Figaro,* which carried some revolutionary implications, and *The Magic Flute,* with its Freemason's humanitarian background, seem to point in this direction. Flashes of political awareness are ascribed to Beethoven and much of his work has been interpreted as revealing certain ideas about the social constitution of mankind.

The instances in which a composer's political engagement manifests itself in real-life action are rare. By far the most decided position was certainly taken by Richard Wagner, when in the year 1848 he engaged most actively in the revolutionary upheavals in Dresden. There is evidence that he not only, on behalf of the Communist rebels, personally ordered the purchasing of explosives and other tools for making bombs but occupied an observation post on a church steeple when the battle between the revolutionaries and the forces of law and order was joined. He escaped persecution but had to live in exile for twenty years. In his later life he worked hard to erase memories of this embarrassing escapade, and after his death his widow Cosima took great pains to expurgate the records, so that the details of this story only recently came to light. But even in his later life, Wagner did not hesitate to dabble again in politics, when he entered in some nearly treasonable negotiations with foreign agents, promoting the elevation of his benefactor, the king of Bavaria, to the German imperial throne. His motivations were quite egocentric, not to say selfish. He was willing to overthrow the royal government in Dresden because they did not appreciate his operas and play them as much as he thought they should. And if his king had become emperor, he would have had more power and riches to lavish on his beloved composer.

In our own time the composer often asks himself whether writing music is a sufficient exertion in a world that seems to require lots of work in order to become livable. Should he at least write articles, give speeches, perhaps run for elective office, or proceed directly to the barricades and fight? Or should he inspire the fighters with exhortative music? Since Wagner's brief revolutionary foray, not many composers were seen on the barricades. But quite a few have reflected their ideas about social and political life in their work in various ways. Whether "absolute" music, that is, music without words, is able to disclose anything of the composer's extramusical thinking is a moot question. But assuming this question is answered affirmatively, deciphering this music's message depends entirely on the explication that its meaning is given. And this, as we know, is entirely arbitrary.

Thus, for instance, it has been said that the most esoteric music, the type represented by Webern and his followers, reveals an attitude of protest against present social conditions, because in its lonely unpopularity it underscores the alienation that has become the curse of mankind. Such identification is of course rather vague and inconclusive. As a matter of fact, music as such does not reveal any specific political ideology or attitude. It is completely neutral. Even if it seems emotionally loaded to the brim, its movement can only be felt or understood as an image of the intensity of the emotion that may have generated it, but never as a likeness of the object of that emotion. Any political or other extramusical implications that a composer may wish to communicate is conveyed by the words he attaches to his music or to which the music is attached.

The most direct way to communicate political views by musical means is through the use of primitive songs and hymns, to be performed by masses of people in order to stimulate or accompany political action. It is obvious that the artistic interest of such materials is extremely low, for its design has to be elementary in every respect. The most effective items were not created by composers of stature but by humble amateurs with a profound feeling for the cause they served and a special flair for the requirements of the style. It is also well known that such tunes may switch party lines with the greatest of ease and serve the adversary just as well, if given the proper lyrics.

On a more demanding level, the most efficient medium combining words and music is, of course, opera because the message that may be carried by the words is drastically strengthened by the impact of dramatic action.

I have written twenty operas, and several of them carry some political implications. For instance, the very first opera I wrote in 1922 (at the age of twenty-two) is in German called *Zwingburg,* which means *The Tyrant's Castle.* It was written shortly after the First World War under the impact of the chaos caused by that war. In those years, following the Russian revolution and the destruction of the imperial governments in Central Europe, there was a great deal of awareness of upheaval and revolutionary change, and some of it is reflected in this opera. I was at that time still a student in Berlin, and a friend of mine, a young doctor who later perished in the gas chambers of Auschwitz, wrote the libretto for me, a very nice but rather amateurish attempt, influenced by the expressionistic playwright Ernst Toller, who had written stage works about the coming up of the masses.

The theme of the opera deals with a people dominated by a tyrant who is never seen. He lives in a castle that also looks like a factory, and his people are forced to go through stultifying mechanical routines. This condition is symbolized in the character of a legendary organ-grinder who was cursed by the tyrant to play his organ ceaselessly, and to the pounding rhythm of this music the people have to perform their jerky motions. In a sudden whim the tyrant decides to liberate the people just for one day. The organ-grinder is tied to a pole so that he can not play his instrument, and the people are free. The unaccustomed freedom drives them into a sort of delirium, and at the climax they decide that even the poor organ-grinder should be set free to partake of their joy. They untie him from his pole and, naturally, he immediately starts to play his machine, signaling the end of freedom. Thus the tyrant was right when he said it would last but one day.

When I had started sketching the music, the Austrian playwright Franz Werfel revised and rewrote this rather pessimistic libretto as a courtesy to me and gave it a more hopeful slant, indicating at the end that salvation was beckoning somewhere in an ever-so-distant future. As much as I appreciated his effort, I found his style a little glib and sentimental for my taste.

The idea of freedom in its many aspects has intrigued me ever since and has become a dominant concept in many of my dramatic works. My second essay for the musical stage, which I wrote only one year later in 1923, and for the first time with my own libretto, was a comic opera called *Der Sprung über den Schatten* (*The Leap Over the Shadow*). There is a German saying (perhaps in other languages too) that nobody can skip over his own shadow, meaning that he can not get over what today is called his hang ups, his personal idiosyncrasies and inhibitions. This idea has haunted me through all my adult life, for I have always entertained wish and hope that I could rearrange some traits of my personality. While, then, this opera was mainly concerned with liberating the individual of his own inhibitions, the political aspects of freedom were not neglected. The principal character was a shy, inhibited poet, hopelessly in love with Princess Leonore, the wife of the ruler of that little principality. His counterpart was an extrovert—a go-getting psychoanalyst who through his treatments made it possible for people to skip over their shadows. The ruling prince was a caricature of ancient aristocracy, an abject debauchee, vile and ridiculous. After much intrigue, masterminded by the doctor, the people overthrew the old regime while the poet was freed of his inhibitions and united with the princess to live happily ever after. Today the most interesting aspect of this rather sophomoric libretto seems to me the fact that it contains a number of motives that I somehow stored away in my mind and picked up many years later. The music of the *Sprung* derives from the then current expressionistic vocabulary, but this is off and on shockingly interlarded with what today would be called "pop" elements.

My next opera, *Orpheus und Eurydike,* was an adaptation of a play by the great Austrian painter, Oskar Kokoschka, at his request. Together with my *Second Symphony* I consider it the most mature part of my early output, but I refrain from discussing it here because the libretto does not directly reflect my own ideas.

Jonny spielt auf, my next operatic effort, certainly does. (An approximate translation of the title is *Johnny Strikes Up the Band.* As to the spelling, it reveals that at that time I knew next to nothing about English or American. I had seen the name "Jonny" in the lyrics of a German hit song and simply accepted it. Later, when Americans thought that an "h" must be missing, I explained that my hero's name was derived from Jonathan.) Here I again took up the problem of personal freedom. The shy poet of *Sprung* became an introvert, problem-ridden composer, and what happened to him was not without autobiographical implications. His troubles were viewed in a larger frame of reference; he was seen as representing the typical mental attitudes of the ponderous, inhibited Central European intellectual. In opposition to him I placed Jonny, the American jazz fiddler, a child of nature, totally free of inhibitions, acting on impulse at the spur of the moment. Obviously the invention of this antithesis was inspired by my first contact with the Western world and my experience of the very evident contrast of mentalities and life-styles between East and West. America, at that time entirely unknown to me, seemed to lend itself most convincingly for localizing the epitome of natural grace and uninhibited freedom that I had in mind. Needless to say, this was an utterly romantic view of America, such as some of the early nineteenth-century writers had entertained. Of course, here the hapless composer is eventually freed of his bondage, and in the railroad station which became one of the several sensational trappings that made this opera famous, he reaches, in the last suspenseful minute, the train that will take him west. He is off to America where he too will live happily ever after—or so we hope.

Political overtones were entirely absent from this opera, which may have been caused by two circumstances. In those years I was living abroad, in Germany and later in Switzerland, and I felt that it was not correct for a foreigner to become engaged in the political problems of the guest country. I felt this way even in Germany, although at that time many Austrians thought that their country was—or better, should be—a part of the great German fatherland. I always had been vehemently opposed to the Anschluss ideology and had emphasized that I was a foreigner in Germany.

At the same time, my interest in political affairs had somewhat subsided. In my adolescence I had developed strong sympathies for left and far left causes, and I have retained them to this day. But I also noticed that the systems the revolutionaries promoted did not exactly recommend themselves as substitutes for what we have here and now. I remember suggesting that, ideally, government should be efficient, noiseless, and inexpensive. Obviously, I was entirely out of tune with reality, for in all three respects the exact opposite has materialized.

My political detachment did not last very long. I gave it dramatic expression in *Das geheime Königreich* which is a fairy tale of my invention and one of a group of three one-act operas written between 1926 and 1928. The king, a lovable but weak character, pressured by his ambitious queen and threatened by rebellion, abdicates and retires to the woods where he will live out his days in communion with nature, because he recognizes the *vanitas vanitatum* of all earthly power. The first of these short operas, *Der Diktator,* reveals a reaction to the phenomenon of fascism which at that time shockingly asserted itself in Italy. The story, however, is again basically apolitical. It deals with an anecdote from the private life of the "strong man" and depicts him as a fascinating though repulsive character. The third of these plays is a short skit, called *Schwergewicht, oder Die Ehre der Nation.* I was prompted to this satire by reading that the German envoy to Washington, on the occasion of an American tour by Max Schmeling or another such hero, had declared that in his opinion the stars of the world of sport were the true ambassadors of the nations, not the scholars and artists. It clearly foreshadowed the coming open season for the egghead-hunters and irritated me a great deal. In my skit I showed the boxing champ as an unmitigated dunce who was cuckolded by his wife with a dancing gigolo while they practiced for a Charleston marathon. In the end he is seen glued to a training machine while a professor from the university appears to present him with an honorary Ph.D. and a high official of the Ministry of Education proclaims him the "pride of the nation."

Soon after my return to my native city of Vienna in 1927, I started working on my next operatic project, *Leben des Orest.* In keeping with the neoromantic fantasies that still inspired my thinking, I wanted now to revive the accoutrements of nineteenth-century grand opera, as we had known them in Meyerbeer and Verdi. Dramaturgically the opera is a tour de force because I compressed into the frame of one operatic evening the whole saga of the Atrides family, which had been treated many times in separate plays—a challenge that tempted me again later. My intention being to bring the colossal story close to contemporary modes of perception, I made it over into a fast moving, violently colorful, folksy spectacle full of anachronisms, the most conspicuous of which was perhaps the somewhat

Italianate music richly sprinkled with jazz idioms. Another anachronism that I mulled over for some time was to bring the wandering Orestes, when he is searching for his sister, Iphigenia, into present-day America whose image apparently still haunted me. I dropped the idea probably because I was not yet ready to handle so outrageously absurd an element. I note this here because the idea surfaced many years later when I conceived *Der goldene Bock*. I have found more than once that the creative mind is peculiarly stingy and hates to waste its outpourings. In retelling the ancient story I took pains to find for most of its miraculous turns second motivations that would make them appear plausible to modern psychological thinking without obliterating their wondrous aspects.

The rising tide of Nazism in Germany, which soon began to threaten Austria too, revitalized my interest in political affairs. It is reflected in *Leben des Orest* mainly in the characterization of Agamemnon as an ambitious führer type whose obsession to become the leader of all Greece by the conquest of Troy is so overpowering that he does not shrink from wanting to sacrifice his son, Orestes, when his villainous relative, Aegisthos, talks him into it. This twist of the ancient story is my invention: Klytemnestra, his mother, saves Orestes by having him spirited away, whereupon Agamemnon, to save face, decides to sacrifice his daughter, Iphigenia, who is rescued by the gods and transported magically to the faraway northern realm of King Thoas.

While in *Jonny spielt auf* contrasts of psychology, lifestyle, character, and temperament were geographically symbolized along an East-West axis, the axis now had turned by ninety degrees to stretch North-South. The brooding, mystical land of Thoas with its snowy darkness and polar storms stood against the straightforward, down-to-earth, colorful *ambiente* of Greece with its brilliant light and permanent serenity.

The concept of freedom is again raised when Orestes,

after being saved from his father, wanders aimlessly about through the Grecian lands and eventually asks himself whether his boundless freedom makes any sense. Responsibility is recognized as the corollary of freedom when Orestes finally is brought to court to stand trial for having killed his mother when he came home and found her an accomplice of Aegisthos in the murder of Agamemnon. The miracle wrought by the goddess Athena by which Orestes is acquitted symbolizes the transition from the ancient matriarchal rule to the new paternal order. Again, this last miracle of the opera is explained rationally without being deprived of its character of divine chance.

To bring in the concept of justification was perhaps the most significant anachronism in my treatment of the story, for it hinted at ideas typical of Christian ethics, such as guilt and redemption. It seems that even at these early portents of the approaching storm I began to see such values in a new, more positive light. But before I made a decisive turn in this direction, I gave vent to my feelings about the political situation in an opera with the title *Cleaning Up Around St. Stephen's* (the saint to whom Vienna's cathedral is dedicated). The story, taking place at the time of the collapse of the old regime in 1918, made satirical fun impartially of all political creeds and principles. I had in mind to write a folk comedy in the Viennese tradition of the nineteenth century, in the spirit of Johann Nestroy, the great satirist whom I much admired. In the tense political atmosphere around 1930 my play was rejected, not unexpectedly, by everybody and never produced, which caused me much anguish. I should have learned from this experience that you cannot count on the people's sense of humor; they prefer to be irritated and exercised.

When the aggressive Nazi schemes against Austria became more evident, I developed a political attitude that today might be called Left-Catholic. Seeing that the liberal and socialistic forces in Germany did not offer any sufficient resistance against the totalitarian onslaught, I imagined that the Catholic substance of Austria, so deeply rooted in its history, would give more protection. I reapproached the church from which I had been alienated since the days of the revolution, and I began to think of a major operatic project that would emphasize my position and strengthen my country in its struggle to maintain its independence. Thus it was particularly inspiring that I was asked by the Vienna State Opera House to write a new work for them.

I chose as subject matter the story of Charles V, the emperor who in the sixteenth century ruled over half of the known world and before the end of his life abdicated, giving away the unprecedented array of power that he had assembled. I had always been attracted by the mysterious antiheroes of the Hamlet type, as they moved through the twilight of history, and my emperor was one of them. Again I was faced with the challenge of condensing the enormous material into manageable size and shape. As emperor of the Holy Roman Empire of the German Nation, Charles had to deal with the religious revolution of Luther and the nationalistic tendencies of the German princes; he had to battle the king of France, who was intent upon rounding out and centralizing his territories; he had to fight the Turks who were overrunning his empire from east and south; he had to deal with popes who had little understanding for the emperor's universalistic dreams; and, as king of Spain, he had to consider the problems arising from the conquest of the recently discovered Western Hemisphere.

Remembering the device used by Paul Claudel in his libretto *Christophe Colomb,* which he wrote for Darius Milhaud, I found a solution by splitting the drama in two layers so that it would be enacted and discussed at the same time. In the sources that I consulted for more than a year, I noticed that the emperor at the place of his retirement, the monastery of San Yuste in Spain, had a painting that Titian had made for him, called *La Gloria,* which is now in the Prado Museum in Madrid. It represents Charles after his death praying at the feet of the Trinity for salvation. This gave me the idea that the emperor, upon receiving the news that his abdication was accepted by the princes of the empire, imagines that the voice of God asks him, from out of the painting, whether he was justified in giving away his power because he thought he had accomplished what God had wanted of him—that is, unite all Christianity under one temporal rule. Thereupon the emperor calls in his father confessor (who, according to the sources, was a young monk of the monastery) and asks him to evaluate his deeds as he recites his life's story. The monk, protesting his ignorance of so formidable a matter as world affairs, consents to listen only after making sure that he would be allowed to interrupt the recital with many questions. The questions that I put in the mouth of the monk are, of course, those I feel a contemporary audience might ask, wondering why we should be concerned with these bygone affairs. At the same time this device made it possible to break the continuity of the story at any point when the monk asked a question. Thus the real drama is the dialogue between Charles and the monk, in which they wrestle with the problem of the justification of the emperor's deeds, while the happenings of history appear as fragmentary illustrations of this dialogue on a different level. This dramaturgical device seemed to be the best way of both condensing the drama to reasonable size and bringing the story into the focus of modern perception, for—unlike *Leben des Orest*—the music would presumably not further this purpose, since I had decided to employ the comparatively esoteric twelve-tone technique.

The very pronounced antinationalistic tendency of the play and its praise of supranational Christian universalism as well as the *kulturbolschewistische* character of its progressive music made it intolerable to the Nazis who even then had already gained enough underground power in Austria to prevent the production of my work at the very opera house that had commissioned it. My own position, which I had stated in many lectures and articles (one of these had the typical title "Conservative and Radical"), had not endeared me to the rulers of Austria either who, while fiercely defending the country's independence, tried to outdo the Nazis in the cultural sector by promoting the worst of moronic provincialism. Knowing that my name was on the blacklists of Germany, where performances of my music were forbidden, and sensing that Hitler would soon take over my homeland, I decided in 1937 to emigrate to the United States.

At that time operatic facilities in this country were practically limited to the Metropolitan Opera in New York, and considering its prevailing negative attitude toward new works, I felt no incentive to write another opera of large format. At Vassar College I became associated with the playwright, Emmet Laver, who obliged me by writing for me a libretto for a chamber opera, entitled *Tarquin*. It fitted well into the line of religiously flavored political thinking that I had developed. The central idea was the confrontation of the dictator with a saintly woman and the tragedy that engulfs both of them. The play had very few characters and I used only six instruments, for we had in mind the creation of something suitable for college workshops. But in 1939 this was an illusion nearly thirty years ahead of reality. Our essay was far beyond the reach of then existing capacities so that the piece was produced only much later in Germany.

Another chamber opera, with only four singers and one instrument (piano), a little drawing-room comedy *What Price Confidence*, with no political but perhaps a few autobiographical overtones, had the same fate, not because it was too difficult, for it was written for a group of singers of the Met who would have easily mastered it, but because the performers never had enough time to give it their attention. Twenty years had to go by before it began to come into its own.

Only after I resumed contacts with Europe, did I again start to think of opera on a large scale. In the early 1950s I wrote *Pallas Athene weint*, an opera with very definite political implications, deriving its subject matter from Greek history. The goddess weeps over the downfall of democracy in Athens at the end of the Peloponnesian war, when Athens is conquered by Sparta, which is depicted as a stronghold of sinister fascism. The story revolves around Socrates and three of his pupils: Alcibiades, a dashing playboy, unscrupulous and reckless, ready to betray his country, go over to the enemy and swing back again, as it serves his ego; Meletos, the old-fashioned type of republican patriot who pretends to stand up for the liberties of true democracy while he actually is undermining them with authoritarian, reactionary schemes; and Meton, a radical pacifist who asks why the Athenians are waging war when they supposedly want peace, and hides in a cave to escape the service.

Some traits of the character of Meletos I saw prefigured in the late Senator Joseph McCarthy. The destruction by unknown agents of the Hermes statues in Athens, as reported by Thucydides in his history of the war, was interpreted as being similar in intent to the burning by the Nazis of the German Reichstag in 1933.

While working on this opera I planned to dedicate it to Adlai Stevenson. But when he became a candidate for President, I felt he would, before accepting my dedication, have to have me carefully investigated, in order to make sure that this was not a Communist scheme to compromise him, and it seemed to me that his staff would have more important things to do. Thus instead of dedicating the work publicly to him, I presented Stevenson with an English translation of my libretto, which I had made especially for him as a Christmas gift, after he had lost the election.

SCENES FROM ERNST KRENEK'S OPERAS

KARL V. Charles V reciting the story of his life to his father confessor, Juan de Regla (left). He describes his arrival at the church at Wittenberg, where Martin Luther (portrait on the backdrop) was buried; far left, Eleonore, the emperor's sister; on the right the duke of Alba. *(Foto Hertha Ramme)*

Charles V and Juan de Regla. Zürich Opera House, 1970. *(Foto Hertha Ramme)*

Pallas Athene Weint. King Agis of Sparta and his queen, Timaea. Hamburg Opera House, 1955. *(Fritz Peyer)*

AUSGERECHNET UND VERSPIELT. Fermando, a young airplane designer, explains to his girl friend, Lucile, how he plans to defeat the roulette game with the aid of the computer.

The pawnshop in the basement of the gambling house. Geraldine, its manager, scrutinizes through an opening between the shelves a customer entering the shop. Vienna, Austria TV network, 1961.

DER GOLDENE BOCK. The Golden Ram carrying Phrixos and Helle, the children of King Athamas, to safety. Over the straits of the Hellespont the girl loses her grip, slides off the back of the ram, and is lost.

The golden ram has arrived among the Navajo and was sacrificed to the gods by Phrixos (left). Chief Chattahoochie and his tribe, who hoped to exploit the precious creature, are indignant. *(Elisabeth Speidel)*

Medea, through Jason's love transformed from a dragon into an Indian princess, reads to Jason what Euripides has her say in his tragedy. *(Jürgen Simon)*

Medea, retransformed into the dragon, jumps onto the roof of the jetliner *Chrysomallos* (Greek for Golden Ram) which is bringing Jason back to Greece. Hamburg Opera House, 1964. *(Elisabeth Speidel)*

Der Zauberspiegel. A thirteenth-century painting representing a Chinese emperor and his mistress (center), the Italian painter who painted himself into the picture (left), and the secret agent of an unnamed Eastern power magically transferred into the picture. *(Foto Sessner)*

The machine that, by reflecting secret rays from a magic mirror, is able to bring dead matter to life is shown with its inventor (left) and the director of the museum that owns the Chinese painting. Munich, Bavarian TV network, 1966. *(Foto Sessner)*

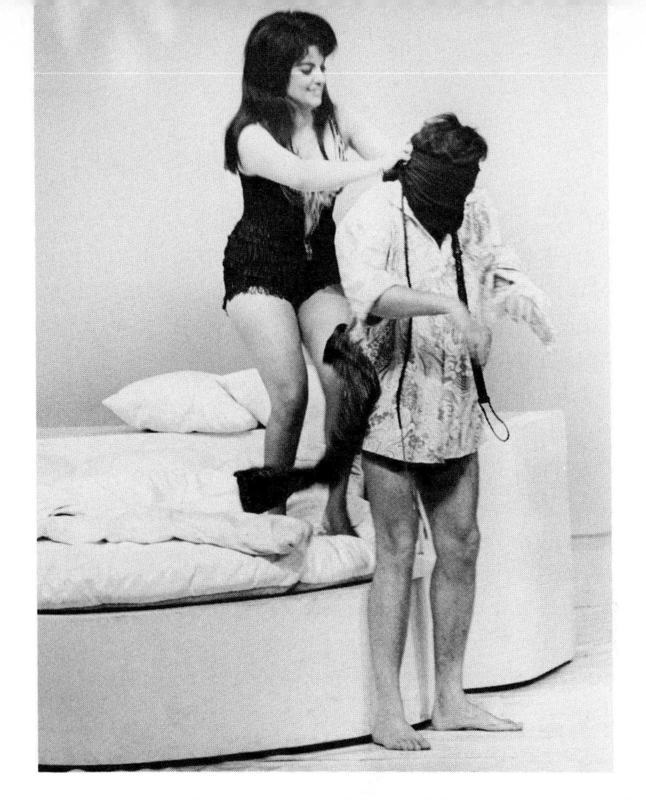

SARDAKAI. Sardakai, queen of Migo Migo, trying to seduce the hooded man whom she believes to be Urumuru, the leader of a rebellion against her regime. *(Conti-Press)*

A beach party including (from left) Heloise, the girl friend of Carlo (center), the poet who wanted to be "engaged"; and Aminta, the friend of the psychoanalyst Adriano. They all become involved with Sardakai. Hamburg Opera House, 1970. *(Elisabeth Speidel)*

The question as to whether a composer should engage in this kind of "message work" probably cannot be answered in a general way. It will depend on his inclinations and his feeling of urgency in regard to communicating his philosophical and political ideas. He ought to benefit from realizing that his musical-dramatic communication will not accomplish any noticeable results in the outside world. Operas, no matter how successful or popular, are patronized only by a small minority of the population, and, if the composer couches his message in the so-called progressive musical idiom, it will be perceived and appreciated only by a still smaller minority within the first one.

It is well known that nowadays revolutions have no chance of success unless they are joined or inaugurated by the armed forces, and the top brass do not usually belong to the opera-going minority nor are they likely to be swayed in their philosophy by hearing atonal music. As a matter of fact, the powers-to-be, regardless of their politics, invariably prefer the thoroughly conformist traditional music that suggests the image of an unshakable, perfect universe in which everything is at permanent rest, because they have to entertain the illusion that the order they have established is perfect and immutable. They distrust any progressive type of music and prosecute its practitioners because such music reflects a higher and more alert status of consciousness and therefore might induce doubt and dissent. Characteristically, the Nazis, under Hitler, promoted exactly the same type of music that was supported by the Soviets in Stalin's period, and both regimes, no matter how diametrically opposite to each other ideologically, were dead-set against atonality and twelve-tone technique, which to the one conveniently symbolized godless communism and to the other bourgeois decadence.

Be that as it may, the composer who realizes the relative validity of his message and its absolute inefficiency will probably have a somewhat detached attitude. Instead of withdrawing into the shell of embittered frustration, he might adopt a kind of active neutralism that in controversial cases tends toward wishing "a plague on both of your houses," although my own earlier experience with this attitude was not exactly encouraging. He might still address himself to the problems of the day, according to his conviction and temperament, like any other citizen, by writing letters to editors and congressmen and by casting his ballot. But in his work he will be more inclined toward viewing the foolish aspects of the whole business.

This mood gained the upper hand when, through my preoccupation with the principles of serial music, I became more and more interested in the philosophical problems of predetermination and chance, of time and space. Two one-act television operas, one written for the Austrian network, the other for the Bavarian, bear witness to this trend. *Ausgerechnet und verspielt* (in German a pun that nearly defies translation) is a comedy dealing with the contest between computer and roulette game. *Der Zauberspiegel* presents an Italian painter who in the thirteenth century is separated from Marco Polo's Chinese expedition and taken in by one of the local sovereigns. When he has a falling out with this lord and his life is threatened, he paints himself into the canvas he is just working at—a portrait of the lord and his mistress. The story switches to the present: a physicist has invented mysterious rays by which dead matter may be brought to life. At the museum they try the rays on the Chinese painting, and sure enough, the Italian painter jumps out of it straight into the twentieth century. Obvious conflicts arise and are resolved only when he decides to repaint himself into his work and the raymaking gadget is eliminated. A peripherical political touch concerns the interest in the rays shown by a commissar of an unnamed Far-Eastern power who has the inventor's laboratory bugged with secret microphones and sends a female agent to seduce him. I noticed that in my short operas I exhibited a penchant for cloak-and-dagger type goings-on. This shows also in two one-act operas that I wrote in the 1950s: *Dark Waters* and *The Bell Tower,* the latter after a short story by Herman Melville.

Der goldene Bock is full-length opera in which attention is predominantly focused on time and space. I decided to use the Greek legend of the Argonauts because it offered me possibilities of roving extensively in both media. The golden ram, created to fly the endangered children of King Athamas to safety, is deflected by some sort of magic, and lands a few thousand miles and several thousand years later in present-day Navajo land. Jason, who in my version is a playboy and antihero, is ordered by his relatives to retrieve the precious golden fleece. But because they enjoin him with a solemn curse not to come back without it, they have to wait for those thousands of years at the gate of Hades. Eventually, Jason finds the fleece guarded by a dragon that, when approached amorously, turns out to be an enchanted Indian princess named Medea. After his American adventure, which becomes increasingly bloody and gory, Jason is finally deported to Greece and delivers the fleece, so that his waiting relatives are allowed to enter Elysium. They have waited so long, however, that nothing seems to make any sense any more. There are many episodes and subplots that bring the story even closer to what has become known as the theater of the absurd.

Obviously, I was no longer taking opera very seriously, and I came to the conclusion that perhaps the theater of the absurd did not have to be invented, for opera as such seemed to be absurd enough. In this mood I conceived my latest operatic effort, *Sardakai,* which was meant to be a lightweight, fluffy farce, poking fun at a few holy cows that happened to stand around. I invented the South Sea kingdom of Migo Migo ("south-southwest of Pago Pago") and its high-strung virgin queen, Sardakai, who was in trouble because of a war for national liberation conducted by her rebellious subject, Urumuru, from his secret hideout in Romadra, a European capital (between Rome and Madrid . . .). When the queen decides to travel incognito to Romadra in order to subdue her adversary by seducing him, she gets involved with two men and their respective girl friends: a psychoanalyst who excels as a ladykiller, and a poet of the "angry-young-man" type who feels that he should become engaged in some revolutionary movement. I realized only later that some traits of these characters were closely related to those of their counterparts in *Der Sprung über den Schatten,* whom I had conceived nearly fifty years before. There are also, again, the conventional trappings of good old *opera buffa*—disguise and mistaken identity. In the process Sardakai not unexpectedly loses both her virginity and her throne, and Urumuru becomes president of the people's republic.

When I was commissioned to write this opera, part of the assignment was to contrive something similar to an arrangement for six singers as in *Cosi fan tutte.* I accepted this as a special challenge, and for additional spice I quoted Mozart by having somebody at a beach party switch on a transistor radio, I had Gluck coming out of a TV set and indulged in similar mischief, giving free rein to a certain impish trait in my makeup.

The opera had not yet been produced at the time of my San Diego lectures. As a postmortem I may add that I had never anticipated the amount of indignation and anguish that the performance, which eventually took place in Hamburg, caused. One could expect the conservatives to be outraged. But they were just as vociferously joined by the radicals on the Left, although in my opera the "people" were victorious after all, and the Establishment inflicted on my engaged poet the ultimate humiliation: that the last refuge where he could indulge in writing a poem was the men's room in a police jail, which I thought was sharp enough an accusation. But they were furious because they felt that I was making frivolous fun of the liberation efforts of the Third World and accused me of being sponsored by the CIA.

Now, at least for a while, I am tired of opera and its political implications.

III

In the early 1920s, shortly after I entered the profession as a diploma-carrying composer, general preoccupation with sociological problems started among the practitioners of all sectors of the musical trade, and it has not subsided much ever since. Undoubtedly, the social revolutions that followed the First World War in the defeated countries, and especially the overthrow of traditional values in Russia, prompted this interest in the social aspects of artistic creation. The role of music in society, its function therein, or the absence of such function are favorite subjects for permanent discussion, oral or printed. It seems that this was not the case in earlier periods. One certainly does not read much about sociological problems in the historical accounts of the centuries before the nineteenth. All that seemed to matter was the artistic quality of the music as determined by the experts—composers, performers, theorists, critics—who measured relative accomplishments by standards immanent to the art itself. Apparently, it was assumed without question that music always had an audience, inasmuch as music was understood to be a form of communication among human beings.

It may be well to notice that a somewhat different attitude seems to have prevailed during the Middle Ages. The symptom of this may be seen in the fact that in the classification of the so-called seven liberal arts, music was grouped together with the abstract arts of measurement and proportion, that is, arithmetic, geometry, and astronomy, which we today would call "exact science," and not with the arts of communication: grammar, rhetoric, and logic. Looking at the formidable complexities of fourteenth- and fifteenth-century music, one is tempted to think that these works were not really meant to be understood or enjoyed by the people who heard them in the same sense as we are accustomed to relate the recipient to the art object he perceives. One might suspect that the ideal recipient of those involuted musical edifices was God, in whose honor also had been constructed those gigantic involutions of Gothic masonry in which that music was heard. Of course, this was religious music, that is, just one sector of the entire realm of music, but it was identical with art music, or what we nowadays call "serious music." The secular music of that age was only marginally affected by the standards traditionally set up for high-level church music, although we have to admit that some of the chansons and other ensemble pieces by composers such as Machaut, Cordier, or Landini were pretty demanding as far as contrapuntal construction and rhythmic complexity are concerned. It is hard to tell what kind of response such pieces found, whether there was any public demand for them in our sense of such terms, or whether they were appreciated by a small minority just like our new complex music today. At any rate, the less exacting specimens of secular music, which would correspond to what we now call entertainment music, certainly had their consumers, as such music always has.

The formulation of the requirement that music ought to communicate something or other and thus evoke a definite response in those who are exposed to it as listeners seems to be a product of the Renaissance. The most obvious result of this change in the psychology of the recipient is opera. Here music becomes the medium through which general human experience is given eloquent articulation in a most immediate form. From here on the listener expects that music will tell him something, be it on the most primitive level (simple acoustical information like the imitation of bird calls, a rhythmic pounding of galloping horses, or other more or less entertaining descriptive tricks), or, on a higher level, supply magic insight into emotional depths that without music might remain obscure. But secular music has not remained operatic. It has become what was called absolute, that is, not explicitly associated with extramusical content, in other words, purely instrumental music without words.

This music has gradually become more and more autonomous. Its changes and developments are dictated by internal evolutionary processes rather than by changes in the expectations of the listeners. Notwithstanding materialistic theories, which try to demonstrate that such changes are being caused by mutations of the social structure, we do not believe that the concerto grosso form, for instance, which dominated the instrumental scene well into the eighteenth century, was replaced by the symphony because of public demand owing to some dislocation in the texture of society. It may be possible from our distant vantage point, however, to discover some parallel evolutionary changes in various fields and ponder the secrets of their synchronization in history. At any rate, secular music has undergone rather dramatic changes ever since the seventeenth century, but its audiences have not modified their expectations that music should communicate some sort of a message to which they hope to respond sympathetically. It must be said also that composers with a very few exceptions, have consistently shared this attitude, which may explain the predicament we experience today.

The predicament arises when the contemporary composer does not have as many paying customers as he wishes to have, and needs to have, to keep alive and active. The protracted discussion of sociological, political, and economic conditions under which the relation between the composer and his public unfolds basically turns on this complaint. Among the numerous explanations offered, the most plausible is twofold: on the one hand, it is a matter of quantity, in that the number of potential music customers has grown immensely during the last two hundred years, while the number of actual listeners has not increased at the same scale; and on the other hand, the composers felt themselves driven to increasingly rapid and drastic changes in their musical language. The size of the potential audience has at least theoretically become identical with the total population of the civilized world, since, after the social upheavals caused by industrial and other revolutions, the consumption of art has ceased to be the prerogative of privileged groups. In the nineteenth century the middle class had set out to emulate the ambitions of the upper levels of society and began to aspire to the enjoyment previously reserved for the aristocracy. In order to satisfy this new and quantitatively increasing demand, the musical world had to develop an adequate organization; and in order to channel music to the new customers the modern commercial apparatus of distribution was created: publishers, concert organizations, agents, opera houses and, eventually, recording, broadcast, and television corporations.

It is the nature of the commercial mind that it will not rest at peace before it has made all potential customers active buyers of the product that it promotes. And for any sales resistance that it meets, it will blame the product for not conforming to the desires of the customer. The fact is that in our century, if not even somewhat earlier, new music did not conform at any given time to the then prevailing tastes of the commercially envisaged, that is, ideally unlimited, set of potential customers. That this seems to have been different in the "good old days" may be inferred, for instance, from the observation that concert programs consisted almost entirely of new compositions. What we nowadays call the standard repertoire, the treasury of well-known, tried and tested war-horses, did not exist. It also still was customary in Beethoven's time for a composer to organize a concert, every year or so, in which he would present exclusively his own works and try to provide added attraction by inserting one or two new items he had written especially for the occasion, much as a painter would mount a one-man show to exhibit his latest creations. This method of presenting a composer's work probably was successful because up to the nineteenth century the musical language had not changed as rapidly and thoroughly as it has since then.

The demand for originality in art seems to have been accentuated in the latter part of the eighteenth century. But the degree to which the originality of the new work asserted itself in relation to the traditional material was limited by the principle that it ought to remain perceivable as a deviation from convention and not as an abrupt and shocking break. In one of his letters to his father, Mozart describes how in his opera *The Abduction from the Seraglio* he depicted the inordinate rage of the character Osmin by assigning the middle section of his aria to a key more remote from the principal tonality than would have been standard procedure for this part of an aria. He adds that he was careful not to choose too remote a key because, according to his aesthetics, even the outrageous must be expressed within the limits of the pleasing and rational. This statement clearly reveals what limitations of his originality a composer was willing to take upon himself, but it also reveals that he was able to expect the appreciation of his finesses by an audience that was so conversant with conventional procedure that it would readily notice even a slight deviation and evaluate its significance.

As the nineteenth century progressed, connoisseurs able to appreciate such wavers were found less and less in a steadily growing general audience. Eventually, such perspicacity has become restricted to a group of experts—mainly the colleagues of the composers, with, perhaps, a few critics and scholars who study his scores with the aid of analyses he has provided. And it is this group that exerts a silent and only subconsciously felt pressure upon the composer, prodding him toward further experimentation, a pressure that augments his own urge to try new, untrodden ways. The customers at large do not push him into the lonely vacuum of which he frequently complains. They do not respond to his innovations, because they are no longer aware of any convention to which the innovations could be related.

The composer frequently comforts himself by rationalizing that he is ahead of his time, that the mentality of the public at large will eventually catch up with him. This way of thinking is supported to some extent by historical evidence. The progressive composers and critics love to quote gleefully devastating contemporary reviews in which composers like Beethoven and Wagner were denounced as imposters, lunatics, and criminals. It is easy now to unmask the perpetrators of such obvious misjudgments as ludicrous dunces, although some of these conservative critics, such as Wagner's Viennese adversary Hanslick, were by no means idiots. Our own reactionary adversaries, however, try to show that the notion of new music being unsuccessful and unpopular with the general audience because it is ahead of its time is a fraud and a fabrication of the sour grapes order, for as they say, really valid new music—such as that of Beethoven and Wagner, for instance—has always been successful even while it was new and in spite of isolated rantings of stupid critics. Probably both viewpoints have merit, and history can, as we have seen, easily be interpreted to support either one with impressive evidence. The term *Zukunftsmusik,* music of the future, coined by Wagner, has become a powerful slogan. Of course he meant not so much that his music would be understood only at some later time, but that he was confident the future would belong to him and his work.

Making modern music a matter of the present instead of the future was attempted during the period of neoclassicism, between 1920 and 1940, approximately. Especially in Germany, the concept of *Gebrauchsmusik,* music for use, gained many followers. It was based on the idea that serious music had become an object of passive admiration rather than of vital concern, that it had alienated the public by requiring it to marvel at its highbrow complexity. The new trend was toward making music instead of listening to it. Consequently, a type of music—Spielmusik—was promoted which could be handled easily enough by a moderately equipped layman. This was music for play, geared to the capacities and tastes of communities of juveniles, such as boy scouts and others, their tools being recorders and guitars. These people were fiercely antiromantic and despised any music written between Bach and Brahms, without noticing that their own aspirations were more romantic than anything else. For what animated them was a dream-picture of the good old days, when society was one big happy family—the lion lying down with the lamb. As an example of such paradisiacal conditions, they liked to cite Johann Sebastian Bach, happily grinding out a new cantata for every Sunday to the delight of an equally happy community of eager consumers. It was conveniently forgotten that he had trouble enough with his board of supervisors who found his music frequently abstruse and unpalatable. The revival of the concerto grosso style was based on the same wishful thinking: that by restoring the outward appearance of seventeenth-century music, one could also restore the harmonious social organization that supposedly had existed at that time and had produced a happy relationship between the composer and his public. Although much of the music generated on these premises turned out to be rather dry, academic, and pedantic, it achieved a remarkable success, especially at the hands of Paul Hindemith. His music has appealed to interpreters who hate really new music but feel guilty if they do not play some contemporary stuff, for its performance does not demand anything beyond the traditional skills and it looks scholarly and sounds modern without being shocking.

Curiously enough, the trials and tribulations that the other contemporary music, the really progressive type, had to endure, eventually brought it to a point where its practitioners too started trying to reach out for a more direct rapport with the listener. During the neoclassicistic era the new music, as embodied in atonality and twelve-tone technique, was severely isolated from the public at large. This was accepted as an inevitable fate in the countries of totalitarian rule, because no matter what their dominant ideology proclaimed to be the truth, they had to repress any kind of art that would reveal and underscore the essentially precarious condition of human existence and encourage protest against existing conditions. But this type of advanced music was not much better received in the so-called free world. It was tolerated but not welcome. I remember having seen an article written by an American music professor, around 1940 or so, in which he explained to his own satisfaction that the German twelve-tone composers were not really driven out by the Nazis; they were, in his opinion, sent by Hitler to America in order to corrupt the spirit of American youth. They only *believed* they were persecuted. In fact, they were secret emissaries of Hitler.

This state of affairs has changed astonishingly during the last twenty years. Not that the attitudes of the famous general audience, the mass of customers, have changed. But within the profession, among the composers, a total about-face took place. The new generation of young composers were no longer interested in the folkloristic or neoclassical exercises of their predecessors. They had discovered Webern and the ideas of serialism. Sociologically speaking, however, not much had changed. This new serial music did not become any more popular with the established institutions than did the music of 1920. It seems that the feelings of frustration caused by this isolation have sparked the introduction of the element of action into the production and performance of music. Music, then, becomes a Happening. It incorporates action of an extramusical nature, which is not only to be heard in its acoustical results but also seen while it is carried out. The listener or witness is encouraged to emerge from the position of the passive recipient glued to a chair and is invited at least to move around or even to participate in some ways in the proceedings. Obviously, such goings-on corrode the traditional concept of the work of art as being a rationally constituted unit of thought, as a premeditated piece of construction. The elements of chance and improvisation take over.

It is clear that an element of protest against traditional values is involved and displays, intentionally, an antiestablishmentarian attitude. No matter how sincerely one might sympathize with such an attitude, the effect is problematical, for even the most outrageous happenings are not likely to bring the Establishment down. In fact they provide the most solid members of the Establishment with sensational titillation. And when the concepts are compared with the more disciplined accomplishments of the nonaggressive kind, they are usually very disappointing in terms of intellectual or any other interest.

Now let us take a look at the machinery determining the social and economic position of the composer. In modern times the source of power in this machinery is the concept of copyright—the principle that the originator of a work of art is entitled to fair compensation by the users of his work, a concept related to the idea of the patent in science and industry. It is a relatively new idea. In the United States, where it is anchored in the Constitution, for instance, it was legally codified in 1790. But it has gained worldwide recognition only in the nineteenth century.

Before the establishment of the copyright principle and the setting up of the organizations necessary to enforce it, the composer usually was compensated for his labors by a one-time fee, or he was on the payroll of a prince or of the church and had to produce and deliver his products to his employer, frequently according to the latter's specifications. Joseph Haydn, for instance, lived and worked during the greater part of his life under these conditions and fared very well. His social status at the court of the princes Esterházy was far from exalted. He ranked more or less on the same level as the chief cook or master of the stable. But this did not prevent him from becoming fabulously successful. It seems that hundreds of his works were printed during his lifetime by numerous publishers in many countries, which is astonishing in itself because at that time there was not a trace of what we today call publicity: no newspaper reviews, no trade magazines, no broadcasts—only word-of-mouth propaganda. Haydn, who had been raised in a prerevolutionary atmosphere, had no complaints about his position. It is remarkable that when he became a free agent after quitting the princely service at the age of sixty he was able to adjust to the conditions of incipient commercialism just as well. But that is another story.

Mozart, a member of a younger generation, was in a much less happy situation. In the first place, it was his bad luck that his employers, the archbishops of Salzburg, were less congenial than the princes Esterházy. It was not only Mozart's natural inclination to chafe under the restrictive aspects of his position but also the unrest of the late eighteenth century which prompted him to kick against the pricks. Gentle of character as he was, he was not very successful in his fight against society. One generation later we see Beethoven, a much more forceful personality, continuing the struggle for a dignified and materially secure position of the composer in society.

Only in our century has the idea of the copyright found general, if reluctant, recognition. It seems hardly believable but it is nonetheless a fact that organizers of concerts, not to speak of proprietors of taverns or nightclubs with musical entertainment, do not hesitate to pay for the use of light, heat, advertising, printed matter, and for the services of the personnel from publicity agent to dishwasher, but find it outrageous that the composer whose music they use wishes to be compensated. Even after the principle of proper remuneration was grudgingly acknowledged, the notion still persisted that royalties were a tip for especially pleasant services rather than a fee for the use of another person's property.

The idea of a systematical exploitation of the copyright became interesting for a composer as soon as his work was likely to have many repeated performances at distant places over indefinite periods of time. Mozart was satisfied to write quickly a new aria for a singer of his acquaintance for a flat fee of a few dollars, in order to pacify the corner grocer who threatened him because of staggering unpaid bills. And the singer would use the aria in her next concert, and then perhaps never again. But when the works of the classics were performed countless times all over the world, their composers did not want to be cheated of their just reward, as were their famous ancestors.

Obviously, it is impossible for the individual composer to control innumerable or even a few performances of his works on five continents. Therefore, from approximately 1900 on, composers and publishers in many countries have organized performing rights societies which develop the apparatus necessary for collecting the monies due to the composers. It is easy to see that this is a business as formidable as it is picayunish, for not only does the society collect from the big symphony orchestras whose programs are published in the newspapers and thus are easily controlled, but also from humble community concerts, where one or two short pieces of a member of the society may have been played, as well as from the innumerable nightclubs where there are no printed programs to reveal how many and which songs were played how many times every night. These monies are collected and also distributed fairly among the members of any one of the various national societies that are tied together by mutual agreements and exchange of their membership lists. The numbers on IBM cards registering all necessary data and channeling the resulting dollars and cents to their rightful recipients have eight and more digits.

On the whole, we have to acknowledge that the performing rights societies are doing a most creditable job. The big money that makes the operation worthwhile, and even possible, results from the mass production and mass performance of entertainment music. But it has been acknowledged within all these societies that so-called serious music, being quantitatively limited in commercial opportunities and qualitatively operating under a handicap, should be subsidized by the lucky entertainer. Very little is heard about corruption or graft in these societies, and their share of annoying red tape is no worse than that of comparable organisms.

In order to have performances controlled by his performing rights society, the composer's music must be available to prospective interpreters, and this is where the publisher comes in. He is in a difficult position because even the most successful composer will inevitably feel that his publisher has not done enough for his work, especially when he notices how some colleagues reach greater fame and prosperity than he does. He will ascribe their success to the inventiveness and efficiency of their publishers and reproach his publisher for not applying these gifts to his own output.

By the way, the notion that the publisher dispenses incredible, perfectly magical powers also exists in the heads of those adversaries of new music who firmly believe that there is a conspiracy of critics, agents, interpreters, broadcasters, and what not, nursed and maintained with the inexhaustible funds of malevolent publishers, for the purpose of cramming down the throats of an innocent public the indigestible modern stuff. Strangely, the question as to why the publishers should waste their riches in this manner when they could make more and easier money by peddling the music that everyone is craving is never asked.

The expectations, which the publisher seems doomed not to fulfill, are based on his peculiar relationship to the work he has acquired. If somebody buys a painting for $10 and sells it for $10,000, the painter who originally sold it does not share the margin, which may appear immoral and outrageous, but it is legal and is accepted as fair. Incidentally, this is why musical works are not interesting as objects for investment—one cannot hang them on the wall or hide them in the basement to wait until the market has gone up. One cannot own a piece of music as one owns a statue. So far the possibility that electronic music can be owned, like a piece of art, has not been investigated. A rich man could commission a composer to produce an electronic tape of which he would be the sole owner, so that whoever wanted to hear this work would have to be invited to do so by the owner.

At any rate, the publisher does not "own" a work as an art dealer does; it is entrusted to him for exploitation, and the composer depends for his income on that exploitation.

The main vehicle for making the musical work a source of income today is the public performance with admission fee. In the old days the sales of printed copies—called sheet music, somewhat disrespectfully in the jargon of the trade—was just as important. Even vocal scores of operas had astonishing sales. I was told by Wagner's publisher that more than 100,000 copies of the vocal score of *Parsifal* were sold during the composer's lifetime alone, which was just a few years after the completion of the work. A percentage of this fantastic demand may be accounted for by the aura of sensation that surrounded the work; but the *Parsifal* score is difficult enough to scare even present-day amateurs, if there were any who would wish to tackle an opera score at all. If our music lovers care to use their fingers, it is more to turn dials or push buttons than to tickle the keys. Thus very few people buy music for solo instruments, chamber groups, or voice. Professional interpreters expect to receive complimentary copies, which they are given in the hope that they will use them in public performance. Sheet music that still sells in large quantities is of the old classical and early romantic period, which owes its persistent popularity to the fact that it is regarded as educational material. Easy choral numbers come under similar headings.

Performances, which have become the main source of revenue as far as new music is concerned, are then the main target of the publisher's promotional activity. The established concert institutions are not a very promising hunting ground since the audiences still demand the same fare as sixty years ago, or at least the managers think so. At that time we were told, as I remember, that the audiences consisted of old people who were reluctant to accept the dramatic innovations of new music. In the meantime one or two new generations must have taken the seats of those oldsters, and yet their attitude seems to be very much the same. If these new audiences held different views when they were young, the establishment apparently has succeeded in assimilating them sufficiently to make them docile customers of the old works.

As far as public performances go, opera productions are the most rewarding financially because opera houses seat lots of people, admission is relatively high, and royalty percentages are adequate. In Europe royalties from broadcasts on radio and television are equally substantial because there these agencies are important users of new music, not so much because their audiences are clamoring for it but because radio and television are conscious of the fact that they render a public service. They are aware of their obligation to serve every sector of the population, even that strange minority group interested in new music, and to support actively the progressive trends in the arts. They not only broadcast this new music, but arrange for public concerts; they organize or sponsor festivals; they commission composers to write new works for them; and some broadcasters have added electronic studios to their imposing list of facilities.

It is hardly necessary to point out that American television and radio have shown no interest in providing these services. We frequently hear expressions of pity for European radio listeners because they are being taxed for their pleasure. Actually, they are not subject to any tax. They pay a very modest license fee, which is no more than a token of appreciation for the service they are getting. If it is customary to pay for a concert or movie ticket, why then should the music we hear from the radio be free? In the United States the public expects radio programs for nothing, because they know that the music they hear, as well as all other programming is offered essentially as bait to keep the listener glued to his machine until the message of the advertiser arrives—the sole purpose of the whole operation. It is peculiar, however, that the listener actually believes that he is getting something for nothing. Whenever the question arises as to whether serious music and opera should be subsidized by public funds, we hear some angry taxpayers protesting that they do not care for opera and do not see why they should pay for the pleasure of those few snobs who pretend to like it. These people seem to forget that they are subsidizing all of radio and television when they pass the checkstand at the supermarket, for the advertisers do not by any means offer these splendiferous spectaculars out of sheer love for their customers, but pass the formidable expenses on to them when they set the price of their commodities. And those who never look at TV have to pay anyway, but, of course, they are a hopeless minority, nearly suspect of subversion.

As we know, there is a roundabout way of subsidizing art through public funds, as long as private money may be used for such purposes, instead of being gobbled up by the tax office. And, perhaps, it is not so bad a system either, because the sponsorship is more diversified and decentralized than under a bureaucratic organization. In one of his conversations with Robert Craft, Stravinsky observed that there is no demand whatsoever for new music and that the agencies that commission new music are buying up surplus symphonies just as governments are buying up surplus wheat and butter, without being at all interested in having these products. I think there is a certain difference. Governments may not be interested in wheat and butter, but they are very keenly interested in the voting power of the masses of farmers that produce those extra masses of wheat and butter. The makers of symphonies and related items are very few and they do not elect the directors of the foundations that are willing to take care of the surplus. It seems there are quite a few people around who are interested in listening to a new serial composition, even by Stravinsky. It is not useful to compare their numbers with those of the Tchaikovsky or Beatles fans. Certainly, their number and buying power are not large enough to maintain the progressive composer in state. Therefore he should not feel guilty for his inability to compete in the marketplace with the purveyors of more conventional material. The minority of those interested in new music is subsidized—*not* the composer. And this minority is a silent one, for whenever new music appears by mistake or miscalculation in the programs of the Establishment, it is the majority of the conformists which pesters the management and the press with complaints and outraged protest. I have yet to read somebody complaining about too much Tchaikovsky or Brahms.

For the last ten years or so, however, new music has gained an "in" position all over the world, not with the established institutions but with a new layer of in-between agencies: festivals, private associations, small groups of performers and listeners, colleges, radio stations, and so forth. I feel that this is a very welcome development, for it is by no means an axiom that any and all music has to be demanded and digested by all people, just as not every book published has to be read by everybody in sight. To call this minority of appreciative listeners "an elite" may not be to its liking, or it may offend those who do not belong to it; it is not relevant, in any event. Even so, its numbers are growing.

Superficially looked at, our period seems to show a bewildering array of completely heterogeneous musical styles. Actually, since 1945, the new international style has become more and more pronounced. Experience reveals that no matter how absurd or provocative a manner of writing appears when new, if it is taken up by more and more composers, it almost automatically becomes more palatable and acceptable to the growing number of recipients. Thus our present silent minority may, as time goes by, eventually achieve a quite different status. Then it will be time to look for something new.

IV

To my knowledge I am the only composer of my generation who has thoroughly and consistently practiced what is called "serialism," and I have been blamed (a) for doing it at all, (b) for doing it too late, and (c) for still being at it.

In order to clarify my position somewhat, I should like to begin by explaining what I understand serialism to be. Discussing this concept today, one feels as though he is talking in a vacuum, for nearly all the early practitioners of this manner of writing music have decided that it has become obsolete. But when these composers developed the ideas of serialism, they said the same thing about the twelve-tone technique while still applying it to their new efforts. Even in criticism being written presently, early dodecaphonic music is still referred to as "serial."

As in so many cases, the confusion is a result of hazily defined terminology. At the present time, it is—or should be—elementary common knowledge that the fundamental concept of the twelve-tone technique is the organization of the tonal material in a set of basic patterns prior to the act of developing individual musical ideas from the material so preorganized, this act being what is understood as "composing music." The preorganization of the material consists of arranging the twelve different pitches (or "pitch classes," for every pitch has a replica in each of the octaves we take into account) available in our tonal system in one of the millions of possible orders of succession. The chosen order, called a twelve-tone row, or series, then becomes the model, mold, germ cell, fountainhead, center of reference, storehouse, or whatever you may call it, from which all that happens in the piece of music is derived. On these grounds, music so composed may be called "serial."

During the first two decades after Arnold Schoenberg had invented this technique and made it public about 1925, only very few composers apart from Schoenberg's personal disciples, Alban Berg and Anton Webern, followed him into this difficult and lonely territory. He did not encourage general knowledge of his new technique, keeping it mainly to himself until his late American years, when he started discussing it in public. During that period neoclassicism of Stravinskyan or Hindemithian observance dominated the world scene of contemporary music, both styles considerably easier to imitate and more promising of tangible success than the twelve-tone technique. As mentioned before, I turned to this compositional discipline around 1930 when I embarked on the project of writing *Karl V*.

To everybody's surprise it came to light at the end of the Second World War that knowledge of the technique spread underground so-to-speak, in spite of the interruption of normal ways of communication, for suddenly numerous young composers turned up all over the world presenting dodecaphonic essays. The most important event, however, was the discovery that a new perspective had been brought into the picture.

It started with the studies of rhythmic modes of medieval music pursued by the French composer Olivier Messiaen. These, in turn, were derived from the prosodic theories of ancient poetry. The idea of setting up groups of durations to be applied to sequences of tones has its prototype also in the isorhythmic procedures of the *Ars nova* of the fourteenth century, when melodic configurations were forced into preestablished rhythmic molds. Eventually, Messiaen and some of his pupils—above all Pierre Boulez and Karlheinz Stockhausen—connected the preorganization of durational sequences with that of pitch successions. This is the beginning of what should properly be called "serial" music. In this light the twelve-tone technique may be seen as one particular province of serialism; but for the sake of clarity it would be desirable to reserve the term "serial" to the music in which the concept of serial preorganization applied to more than just one aspect of the musical process.

As frequently happens with new notions of great consequence, these ideas were "in the air" and ready to materialize wherever alert minds could sense them. The American composer, Milton Babbitt, had already in the 1940s written music in which the manipulation of time series was integrated with dodecaphonic procedure, but nobody paid much attention to such endeavors. While in Europe innovations of this kind are quickly formulated in "manifestos" and widely discussed in all coffeehouses (which admittedly have some drawbacks), in the United States they are more or less ignored because of the low esteem in which intellectual pursuits are generally held and because there are no coffeehouses of the kind found in Europe.

Eventually the idea of arranging series of discrete, numerically measurable values was applied to other, and possibly all aspects of music: dynamics, register, density, timbre. The young composers introduced the term "parameter" to designate these variables. It is symptomatic of the general frame of mind of this generation that they loved to use in their theorizing a terminology borrowed from the exact sciences, even when they did not understand it correctly, as was pointed out by horrified mathematicians and physicists. It reveals a tendency toward detaching music from traditional emotional implications which were felt to be embarrassing. This too has precedents. We remember that music in the medieval classification of the arts was listed among the sciences of proportion and measurement, instead of the arts of communication.

When after an absence of thirteen years, I began to

travel to Europe in 1950, I had, among other engagements, an invitation to give lectures and seminars at the summer music institute in Darmstadt, and there I became more thoroughly acquainted with serialism. I glady confess that I actively approached this technique motivated chiefly by curiosity, and in my opinion there is nothing wrong with this. Progressive composers have routinely been blamed for experimenting with new ideas, new sounds, new instruments, new techniques, new designs "just for newness' sake," instead of being driven to it by "inner necessity" or, probably still better, not at all. I feel that it is perfectly legitimate for a composer to look for something new and different just because it is new and different, and he should stop apologizing for being curious.

I realized that in my *Twelve Variations* for piano and my *Sixth String Quartet*, written in 1936 and 1937 I had touched upon expanding dodecaphonic procedure in a new direction by programming the distribution of the forty-eight basic shapes of the twelve-tone row over the total area of the composition. This might be interpreted as foreshadowing serial procedure, because here a so-to-speak abstract ordering of elements of the material other than single pitches is precompositionally imposed upon the overall design, determining in advance what configurations of tones will appear at certain points or areas. But at that time I seemed to have reached, in these works, a technical saturation point, and I did not continue on this track. As a matter of fact, during the 1940s I tested various methods of relaxing the structures of the twelve-tone technique, not foreseeing that a principle I discovered in those essays and which I called "rotation" would become one of my most productive tools once I joined the serialists.

After my "relaxing" period, I was obviously ready for a new encounter with that redoubtable complexity which seemed to be the most durable characteristic of atonal music, and I sensed that serial preorganization of the parameter of time would produce new heights of complexity.

At the same time I became acquainted with the newly discovered potentialities for musical composition in the electronic medium. Apart from offering new, so far unheard-of sound qualities, its main attraction was the possibility of obtaining degrees of rhythmic accuracy that could never be demanded of even the best trained live musicians, and that certainly would lure composers intent upon complexity of texture and design.

In my first electronic essay—the first section of a religious work *Spiritus intelligentia, sanctus*—I constructed an interlude of about three minutes. It is, technically speaking, a double canon in that two tone-lines run off simultaneously with their imitations. The fact that these imitations occur not only at different pitch levels (as in the classical canon) but also at different speeds represents an increment of complexity owed to the property of electronics, for rerecording a given tape at a different pitch level at that time automatically changed the speed of the recorded sounds. To predetermine the durations of the individual tones in the tone-lines, I reduced certain measurements applying to the length of the whole interlude proportionately to fit the much shorter phrase units of the canon. The duration of sounds was expressed in centimeters of tape, which in those days was running at the extremely high speed of 76 cm. (30 inches) per second. At the beginning of the canon my "time series" showed spans of 48, 107, 59, 9, 80, 45, 8, and 156 cm., which, if combined with one or two more strands having similar time spans, results in a degree of rhythmic complexity that leaves little to be desired. If these stretches of tape are expressed in standard clock time on the basis of 76 cm. per second, we obtain the following time values: 0.63, 1.4, 0.77, 0.118, 1.05, 0.59, 0.105, and 2.05 seconds. Not only is it impossible to represent such a sequence of time values by means of conventional notation or to devise for the purpose a manageable new notation but, above all, accurate execution of these fractions of seconds is absolutely beyond the capacity of live musicians. Yet cutting 48 cm. from a tape on which the first sound was recorded, 107 cm. from the second tape, and so on, and splicing these pieces together is a childishly easy, if laborious and inordinately time-consuming operation.

Going one step further, I was looking for some principle by which time values to be assigned to the sounds could be derived from the twelve-tone row that still was considered the ideal center of reference for the whole work, the powerhouse generating all impulses that would innervate the remotest details of the piece, the nucleus containing in embryonic shapes all gestalt to be developed in the course of the composition. To think of the work as a unified musical universe unfolding from one basic figure according to one all-permeating law derived therefrom was a philosophical concept inherited from the founding fathers, hallowed and not subject to doubt.

Because time measurements had to be expressed in numerical values, it was necessary to find such values in the tone-row. The only feature of the row that obviously lends itself to the purpose is the intervals between the successive tones. These may be measured in terms of the half-steps they comprise (for instance, reading upward: D to F = three half-steps, namely: D to D-sharp to E, E to F; or D to A-flat = six half-steps, D to C-sharp = eleven half-steps), or by taking into account the ratios of successive frequencies (2/3 for the fifth, 3/4 for the fourth, and so on). I preferred the first method because I wanted to write music for human interpreters and the second method seemed again to produce fractions that were too complicated. At the same time I was aware of the danger that a consistently straightforward coordination of tone- and time-patterns might lead to permanent recurrence of identical situations and thus create undesirable repetitiousness.

The solution was suggested by the principle of "rotation" that I had tentatively developed years before. Since the term "rotation" in later serial theory was used to describe certain procedures involving graphical motions of notational shapes on the music paper, my device should perhaps more correctly be called a special form of permutation. In my choral work *Lamentatio Jeremiae Prophetae,* written in 1941, I divided my tone-row in two scalelike six-tone groups, and from each of these groups I derived five additional patterns by putting consecutively the first tone of each at the end of the next. Of course, all six patterns would contain only the same six tones. I derived another set of patterns by transposing the five new ones to begin with the initial tone of the original. This process would gradually introduce the six tones left out in the first set (fig. 1).

As pointed out earlier, this concept was meant to relax the rigidity of the twelve-tone technique, as I had known it thus far. In my new system of patterns I could occasionally use only those having the same six tones or, at will, add one or more of the other groups to enlarge my pitch resources. Thus I felt I could develop a richer palette of harmonic hues, a greater variety of characteristic sounds than when I was forced to constantly use all twelve tones, and yet remain faithful to the basic tenets of the technique. In other works of the 1940s I used this escape hatch by applying the rotational device to groups of less than six tones. Obviously, this leads soon enough to giving up the twelve-tone mechanics entirely. The resulting music sounded "twelve-tonish" because my mind was steeped in this style from the many years of practicing it. I came to the conclusion that arriving at this kind of "liberated" music was perhaps the real purpose of having experienced the stricter forms of dodecaphony.

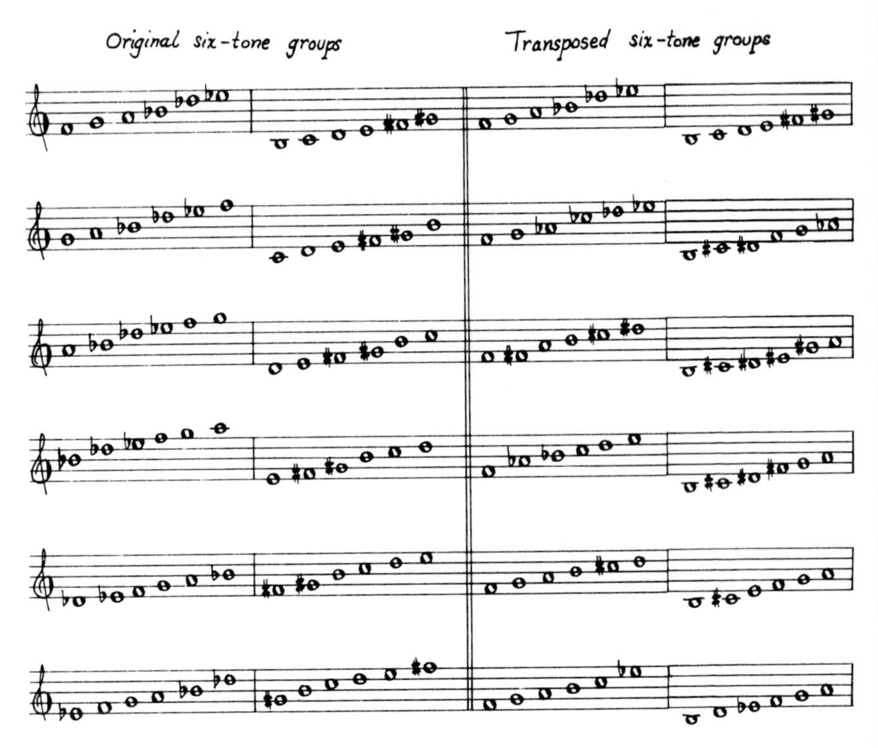

When, in the 1950s, I felt the urge to undergo a new discipline, it turned out to be much stricter than the old one. To begin with, I elaborated on the idea of rotation, setting up derivative forms of the series by having adjacent tones systematically switch their places. To illustrate: when the original order of the tones was

1 2 3 4 5 6 7 8 9 10 11 12,

I would build a secondary row, reading

1 3 2 5 4 7 6 9 8 11 10 12,

followed by

3 1 5 2 7 4 9 6 11 8 12 10,

and

3 5 1 7 2 9 4 11 6 12 8 10,

and so forth. If a mild pun is permissible, one might call this procedure "progressive retrogression." I applied it in an orchestral composition *Kette, Kreis und Spiegel,* in which I again carefully programmed the distribution of these derivative rows throughout the whole work, which resulted in some curious structural symmetries I might not have thought of, without this planning.

Only now I felt ready for total serialization of all parameters. In 1957 I was invited to hold the Christian Gauss Seminars in Criticism at Princeton University, and when I discussed serial composition, Professor R. P. Blackmur, who faithfully attended all sessions, brought to my attention the ancient poetic form of the *sestina,* which I had not known. It fascinated me a great deal, and I decided to use this model of poetic structure as a diving board for the plunge for which I had prepared.

The sestina is a poem of six stanzas, each of which has six lines. The words that stand at the end of the lines are the same in each stanza, but their order of succession changes. If it is in the first stanza

1 2 3 4 5 6

it will be in the second

6 1 5 2 4 3,

in the third

3 6 4 1 2 5,

in the fourth

5 3 2 6 1 4,

in the fifth

4 5 1 3 6 2,

and in the last

2 4 6 5 3 1.

It is easy to see that one more application of the same switching principle will lead back to the first sequence.

The music of my *Sestina* is based on a twelve-tone row divided into two groups of six tones each.

The figures indicate the number of half-steps within each interval. These six-tone groups now are rotated according to the principle of the sestina so that the second A- and B-groups read:

The next permutation is:

and so forth. The tones are always placed so that they will stay within the range of the original form and the intervals are so measured up or down that their magnitudes will not exceed the figure 6. Thus the sequence of these magnitudes constantly changes as a result of the permutations of the tones.

The durations of the tones of the whole work are derived from these magnitudes in the following manner: each magnitude corresponds to a time segment containing as many time units as the interval figure indicates. Consequently, the first time segment has four units, the second three, and so on. Each segment has as many tones as it has units. The duration of these tones is determined by a subdivision based on the same sequence of magnitudes. If the first segment has four units and four tones, its subdivision is based on the first four values of the original row: 4 3 1 6. The sum of these being 14, the subdivision unit for the first segment is 4/14. The duration of the tones within this segment now are determined by multiplying 4/14 consecutively by 4, 3, 1, and 6. The durations, then, are 16/14, 12/14, 4/14, and 24/4 of the basic value.

To facilitate computations each basic unit is assumed to contain ten micro-units. We arrive at the subdivision of the first segment by dividing 40 (four times ten) by 14. The result is 2.85. This number is multiplied consecutively by 4, 3, 1, and 6. The results are 11.40, 8.55, 2.85, and 17.10. If the work had been realized in the electronic medium, these values could be produced with utmost accuracy. Because it was conceived for live performance, the time values were adjusted as follows: 11.5, 8.5, 3, and 17. If the smallest numerical unit (0.5) is represented by a thirty-second note, the rhythmic shape of the first four tones is:

(Actually in my composition these time values are much shorter because other serial considerations entered the computation; the procedure is far too complicated to be demonstrated here. Another marginal remark: contrary to common belief, knowledge of higher mathematics is no prerequisite for this kind of work, only infinite patience. Some of the results are startling and rewarding.)

"Density" is the next parameter to be determined serially. There are six degrees of density. In "density 1" two tone-groups run off simultaneously, the durations of the individual group being determined by the mechanism described above. In "density 6" twelve such strands run off at the same time. Another parameter regulated serially is the location of the tones within the gamut of six octaves designated as the *ambitus* of the work.

The structural layout is so devised that each "rotated" version of any six-tone group will combine once with every other. Thus the music of the first stanza is based on the first statement of the A-group, which in each subsequent line of the stanza is combined with one of the forms of the B-group rotated from B 1 to B 6. The second stanza has A 2, combined again with all B-groups, but now in a different sequence, according to line 2 of the sestina pattern: B 6, B 1, B 5, B 2, B 4, B 3, and so forth

It is characteristic of all these operations that systems of invariable magnitudes are, according to plan, constantly combined with continually changing sets of magnitude, so that new situations constantly arise. Whatever happens in the course of the work is the result of predetermination, but at the same time because of its complexity, largely unpredictable, except perhaps if the relevant information were fed into a computer. To illustrate: if the succession of tones is determined by serial regulation (as is the case in the "classical" twelve-tone technique) and, in addition to this, the timing of the entrance into the musical process of these tones is also predetermined by serial calculation, it is no longer possible to decide "freely" (that is, by "inspiration") which tones should sound simultaneously at any given point. Whatever happens in this parameter is a product of the preconceived serial organization, but by the same token it is a chance occurrence because it is as such not anticipated by the mind that invented the mechanism and set it in motion. The unexpected happens by necessity.

The dialectical cohabitation of predetermination and chance appeared to me as one of the essential features of serialism in music. It is the dominant idea of the poem that I wrote for my *Sestina,* and it has haunted me ever since. Having tasted blood, I applied what I had learned in the *Sestina* with a vengeance in an orchestral work with the Latin title *Quaestio temporis*—a question of time. The computations required for the determination of time values follow principles similar to those of the *Sestina,* but they are more involved. Many of these intricacies are due to exploiting the arithmetical implications of the numerical difference between 11 and 12, for in this work I used a tone-row that not only included all twelve pitch classes but also all eleven intervals available within an octave.

The idea of the "all-interval" series had preoccupied me ever since I started working in the twelve-tone technique, and I consulted many mathematicians about a formula for constructing such tone-rows. They usually smiled indulgently at so elementary a problem, then declared that it would take a little more thinking, and after that were not heard from again. The problem has been solved by some elaborate mathematical operations described by Herbert Eimert in his definitive book on serialism. When I discussed it in the 1940s with my physicist friends at Los Alamos, they found it to be perfect nourishment for the early computer they were building. Since then properly programmed computers have solved it mechanically in various places and have furnished complete tables of all conceivable all-interval rows.

One of the most important insights gained from my serial work was that this technique radically changed the character of our music. Since music in the age of the Renaissance had acquired communicative functions, listeners developed the habit and consequently the urge to interpret musical phenomena to which they were exposed as communication of sentiments and ideas. Music was understood to be some kind of language, and in its structural properties it took on many characteristics of speech. Theorists began to use such terms as "phrase," "sentence," "period," "question and answer," "subject," and "logic." The perfect musical work was seen as having a clearly defined theme that was logically developed, a structure that could be followed from point to point, from beginning to end.

The first symptom of music's alienation from its speechlike tradition may be seen in the emergence of the concept of retrogression in later twelve-tone music. While the systematical layout of the roster of available forms of the tone-row calls for the introduction of its retrograde, the notion of turning around not only the tone-row as a basic element but also complete musical ideas, even building circular structures that would run back into their beginnings, was developed by Webern and other, later dodecaphonists. I have written a number of such pieces. Retrogression is foreign to speech as well as to speechlike music since 1600; palindromes are contrived only as hilarious stunts; canons in *cancrizans* mode are rare and were put together mainly to exhibit erudition. In medieval music, however, retrogression is an entirely familiar device. In modern use it takes on some vaguely philosophical undertones because it seems to suggest that time might be reversible.

Because in serial music gestalt is the result of orderings made prior to its creation, the freewheeling inspirational invention of "themes" is virtually impossible, which also eliminates the concept of "development." Thus the perception of serial music rests upon different premises. The interest that it evokes emanates from what it has to offer at any moment rather than from a context that may be followed intellectually by the listener's retaining in his memory musical shapes and profiles to be recognized later on. It is therefore, contrary to common belief, intellectually much less demanding than traditional music. Whatever structural features the listener seems to observe is a product of his own mental processes. In this sense it requires more imaginative participation than the old music, but it probably also stimulates the imagination to a higher degree. I realized that the "athematic" quality of serial music was for the younger composers perhaps the strongest bait when they were caught in the serial net, because serialism was the most secure way of preventing relapse into traditional routines. It should be mentioned here that the Czechoslovakian composer Alois Hába promoted and practiced athematism in the early 1920s, even before the twelve-tone technique came to light.

With *Sestina* and *Quaestro temporis,* I had reached a point of saturation similar to that experienced in the twelve-tone technique with my *Variations* and the *Sixth Quartet.* But now as then this did not suggest to me that I had exhausted the possibilities of serialism and should turn to something else. I became rather interested in exploring further variants and ramifications of the serial concept. My younger colleagues apparently felt otherwise, and in their circles it has become fashionable to decry serialism as obsolete, or even a dead-end road that should have been avoided. The alarming rapidity with which in our age artistic innovations are dismissed before they have reached fruition seems to be due to the hectic pressure exercised by public opinion. I remember seeing, a few years ago, a newspaper report about one of the international music festivals headlined: "So-and-so Festival—No New Breakthrough." It must be very depressing for the composers represented there to read that they disappointed the critic because they did not stand on their heads to signal a "breakthrough." Unfortunately, many of the young composers seem to have decided to do just that. It is regrettable that a new style is not allowed to mature and to unfold its potentialities. We are not aware that anybody pestered Franz Schubert to "break through" the late Beethoven, although he was twenty-eight years his junior. His music was bold enough as it was.

In subsequent serial works I tested various applications of premeditated measurements, off and on, leaving some parameters open to free manipulation while strictly ordering others. A group of small pieces for two pianos has the title *Basler Massarbeit*, which in German is a double entendre because *Massarbeit* means both "measured work" and "custom made," and these pieces were written for two friends of mine in Basel, Switzerland. Here the subdivision of the bars, resulting from maneuvering a preconceived time-series, became gradually more complicated and, being different for each of the two instruments, made the execution very tricky—almost impossible without an optical metronome.

Sechs Vermessene is the title of a set of six piano pieces, and another pun, for "vermessen" means not only "strictly measured" but also "presuming." It recalls one of the lines of my *Sestina*, which reads: "Is it presuming to force such an extent of measure on life?" In these pieces I stressed the aspects of applying different time patterns to different layers of varying densities. Seeing that preorganization of pitch- and time-successions was leaving the parameter of simultaneities (in traditional terminology: harmonies) indeterminate, I tried in one of the pieces to start with predetermination of just that parameter: constructing from the tone-row a basic material of fifty simultaneities and then organizing these according to preestablished series of time and dynamics. I took this experiment up again on a larger scale in an orchestral work, *Perspectives*. The title of this composition suggests that various musical configurations arranged in layers are combined at several different levels of dynamics and speed, the perspective idea being further emphasized by having some of the elements played offstage.

Similar conceits prevail in another orchestral work called *Fivefold Enfoldment.* The paradox that the composer, by most rigorously planning every move in certain areas is giving up control over others, increasingly focused our attention on the factor of chance. It has become dominant in a great deal of so-called post-serial "aleatory" music. But I have never wished to surrender my freedom to invent in favor of some chance mechanism, like throwing dice or flipping coins, because I still find even laborious serial computations more interesting than such primitive exercises. I did become interested in devising musical works in which the interpreter was given multiple choices of combining materials that in themselves were totally worked out by the composer. This procedure seems to reflect a very characteristic trait of the contemporary mind, which is rather skeptical of categorical statements and prefers a pluralistic view allowing for more than one solution to a given problem.

Along these lines I wrote the *Fibonacci Mobile* for string quartet and piano. It consists of a number of elements whose durations are proportional to the numbers 2 3 5 8 13 21 34. They are a part of the so-called Fibonacci series in which each number is the sum of the two preceding ones. These elements may be combined—that is, played simultaneously in many different ways—and a performance of the work should present several such combinations, so that their differences may be appreciated. The effect should remind one of the aspects of a spatial mobile that, by turning about, shows its elements in constantly changing perspectives.

The orchestral piece *From Three Make Seven* is of similar nature. Here I composed serially two blocks of music of forty-two bars each. They are based on a twelve-tone row and all their time measurements are painstakingly worked out. There are two condensed versions of either one of these blocks, one of twenty-eight, the other of fourteen bars, which means that the same musical material runs off so much faster and has higher density. Furthermore, each of these blocks is available in three different orchestrations: for wind, string, and percussive instruments. These eighteen elements have seven points each at which they may be synchronized. Obviously, countless possibilities exist, and again several of them should be presented in preference. But the selection has to be made beforehand and abided by; nothing is left to improvisation.

There have been objections that this project does not make any sense because the results of the combinations are utterly beyond control, and if the unavoidable chaos was intended, the serial preparation of the material was useless —one could just as well let everybody play at will. This is, of course, not true. Since the elements are derived from the same substance, they are very closely related in every detail, and many of the possible combinations yield surprising coincidences, correspondences, contrasts, and other relationships. One might say that the arrangement represents a sort of variations, but of a kind a composer could hardly conceive without sluicing his inventions through the involuted system of serial channels.

In some later works, as for instance in *Horizon Circled*, I tried to introduce a certain degree of chance into an otherwise strictly determined design. Here the piece is divided into time segments (bars) comprising from one to eleven time units (beats) of equal length. The number of units in each segment corresponds again to the magnitude of the intervals of the basic tone-row. All twelve tones of this row or its rotational derivatives are sounded in each segment, which causes the density to vary considerably. The time points at which the tones are to be played within each segment are not precisely defined but only indicated in relation to other tones. The players are instructed to play their tones approximately, according to the graphic position of the notes in the segment. The purpose of the arrangement is to remove from the music all traces of "squareness" and to obtain a floating character. There are other passages to be played "as fast as possible," strings of random pitches following approximately a graphic outline, and the like.

The emphasis placed upon the element of chance has eventually led to a new golden age of improvisation, including all problematical aspects thereof. Obviously, the improvisation in post-serial music is expected to produce a certain stylistic image that will be destroyed if some mischievous or lazy players would "improvise" broken D-major triads. It requires well-intentioned, dedicated, and congenial players so steeped in the style of the composer (who becomes more and more an instigator of vaguely delineated musical activity) that they could almost write the music that he omitted putting down on paper. Even in such lucky circumstances, experience has shown that musicians in the heat of the battle are likely to fall back onto what they know and remember best, what comes naturally to their fingers. More than once I have heard a composer complain that "they did not improvise correctly"; if he knew so well what would have been "correct," it would have been best for him to write it down. To prevent group improvisation from becoming dull, or missing the stylistic image, more or less detailed instructions and guidelines have been resorted to, and the results tested in practice run-throughs. But obviously rehearsed improvisation is a contradiction in itself. In many cases it appears that this kind of activity may be relatively satisfying, or at least entertaining, for the participants, but is rather disappointing and boring for those invited to hear the results.

Something akin to improvisational attitudes has developed in the field of composition in the electronic medium. While one of its initial attractions was the possibility of obtaining otherwise inaccessible degrees of accuracy in time relations, it later became the extraordinary capacity of this medium to develop new sound qualities that absorbed the attention of composers. Since rhythmic subtlety accomplished through ever more complicated serial computations served the purpose of making sure that the result would sound chaotic, we learned that this character could be achieved by simpler means and serial organization reserved for other purposes. Moreover, the fact that electronic generators will produce any conceivable frequency freed us from the limitations of the twelve-tone system.

The composer, having a general idea of the total structure of his project and the distribution of fields of sound therein, "improvises" on his machinery, experimenting with sounds, selecting what seems useful in terms of the image he has in mind, rejecting or putting in storage what does not fit his concept. Thus the work emerges gradually from more or less fully realized passages by filling in what seems to be required for contrast or transition, adding here, cutting out there, adjusting prerecorded elements—in other words, doing things that are reminiscent of rather old-fashioned ways of composing music, except that they do not take place on paper. This activity is related perhaps to creating an abstract painting. But whatever importance is attached to its improvisational component, its result is definitive. What is recorded on the tape is *The Work*, with no allowance for indeterminacy or chance—unless the tape is further electronically manipulated in performance, which would simply mean that the product as furnished by the laboratory was only partly finished and designed for applying various additional improvisational finishing touches. The notion that the product delivered by Beethoven is not finished either because it is exposed to innumerable interpretations does not hold good, for these interpretations do not attack its substance—at least we hope this is so.

Some composers, especially beginners venturing into

the field of electronics, become so infatuated with the exciting unheard-of sounds they are able to produce, they overlook the fact that the most sensational acoustical phenomena are only material which fails to hold the listener's interest unless it is used in a more demanding context. If the experience of serialism has eliminated ability or inclination for traditional structural design, it simply means that composing interesting music has become so much more difficult because something else has to take over the role of contextual variety and continuity, which seems to be indispensable if the listener is to be kept awake.

Personally, I found certain combinations of electronic elements with live instrumental and vocal materials to be a particularly attractive way of using the medium. The impersonal quality of electronic sound and its startling potentialities of formidable amplification add unexpected monumental grandeur and gripping dramatic contrast to the humane character of instrumental and vocal sounds. In such combinations, electronic sound is also better suited to public performance than in its pure form, which seems to favor private reception over the radio or from a tape recorder.

Here I should like to mention a piece for chamber orchestra and electronic sounds, called *Exercises of a Late Hour.* Its orchestral parts offer a brief survey of dodecaphonic procedure progressing from the most elementary run-through of the twelve-tone row in unison and equal meter to the more involved canonic structures, in confrontation with the improvisatory spontaneity of the interweaving electronic elements.

Another work in which I exploited the polarity of live and electronic sounds is *Quintina* for voice, six instruments, and tape. Here I applied the rotational principle of the *Sestina,* reduced, however, from six elements to five. While the poem I wrote for the earlier work deals with the dialectic interrelation of total predetermination and unpredictable chance, I contemplated in the *Quintina* the alienation of language and music. Again the instrumental passages are premeditated according to the procedure discussed for *Horizon Circled,* with the difference that here the time segments have only one to five units; the intervening and overlapping electronic sections show the free articulation germane to this medium.

It is probably partly owing to the observation that much of post-serial music must offer stimuli over and above what it can do by acoustical means to keep the recipient's attention in focus, and partly because group improvisation frequently approaches the character of a parlor game, that eventually the visual aspects of musicmaking are stressed, so that it becomes a "happening," a multifaceted slice of life. Undoubtedly, this tendency reveals pronounced hostility toward a frame of mind in which art is considered a realm separated from ordinary life and revered for its being exempted from the viscissitudes to which undistinguished mortals are exposed. It has been little noticed that such an attitude is not far removed from the reactionary pre-Nazi mentality of promoting *Spielmusik,* togetherness, and craft instead of art. But while value was attached to skills that had to be learned, the encouragement of do-it-yourselfers to do your own thing tends to equate the creation of music with unskilled labor. Whether audiences are invited to walk around during performances and to pay only casual attention to the music played (which has been practiced in "promenade" concerts and public parks since time immemorial), or to participate in it by making noises on homemade tools; whether traditional instruments are abused in outrageous ways and possibly destroyed for good measure (which once was known as students' pranks); whether obscenities are sung or shouted and customers in the audience molested from the stage—the intention always is to divest the art of that solemn dignity behind which it was hiding and which is considered hypocritical and standing in the way of progress toward more humane social conditions.

It is entirely possible to sympathize with the destructive tendency revealed in these exercises and to dream of starting over again with a clean slate. So far, the anti-art manifestations are being evaluated on the terms of legitimate art, and on this basis they mostly are found wanting. The revolting nuisance is meant to produce a shock by taking place where the exalted had been held in awe, but by comparison it usually appears inane. The piano into which a can of peas is poured is the same on which we only yesterday heard Beethoven, and on the wall where we used to see Rembrandt hangs a toilet seat. The shock wears off quickly. But when anti-art relinquishes its aggressive ambitions and blends into the shapeless mold of everyday life, it soon takes on the character of decorative art, like wallpaper, or the music we hear in elevators and supermarkets, or it becomes shallow entertainment. While we may visualize with equanimity a world without public consumption of "serious" music, we doubt that the multimedia exertions will offer a satisfactory substitute.

The Composer Views His Time

by JOHN L. STEWART

> Das Unvermessene bedarf der Zahl,
> im Ungezählten missen wir das Mass.
>
> (The unmeasured stands in need of number,
> in the unnumbered we miss measure.)
>
> —ERNST KRENEK, *Sestina* (1957)

The world esteems Ernst Krenek as a composer, yet it might have known him as a man of letters: a dramatist, poet, short story writer, and essayist with strong views about the "unmeasured"—the disorderly and too often meaningless—conditions of his time. For throughout a career of astonishing productivity he has been all of these. Indeed, in 1930 he almost gave up composing for literature and journalism. Along with sixty-seven musical works that had brought him international fame and considerable means, he had by then written the libretti for six of his eight operas, the verses for two long song-cycles, and numerous essays on the musical and social scene. In recognition of his gifts as a writer and observer of his milieu, he had been invited by the literary editor of the *Frankfurter Zeitung* to contribute essays, sketches, and book reviews to what was then widely regarded as the best newspaper in Germany. As he remarks in his first essay, he had come to a dead end with his music, having exhausted the neo-Romanticism that had engaged him since 1924. Only after long deliberation, during which he was fully aware of the gravity of the issue, did he decide to make a new beginning in music with the twelve-tone technique. But his interest in writing was undiminished, and in 1932 he helped to found *Dreiundzwanzig* (better known as *23*), a satirical journal to which he contributed many pieces until it suspended publication in 1937. In fact, writing has continued right down to the present to be of nearly equal importance to him, and by now his collected poems, plays, and essays fill five substantial books and eight booklets.[1] There are, as well, many uncollected pieces whose continuing relevance warrants republication. Most of his writing has been done in German, but the pieces in English have an enviable idiomatic ease amounting at times to raciness. All show wit, acumen, and a flair for generalizations qualified by an appreciation of the abundance and variety of life. By turns playful and profound (and often both) Krenek is a shrewd commentator on human behavior and some of the fundamental problems of the age; the quality of his writing suggests that had he chosen to devote to letters alone the awesome imaginative power that he has expended upon a much broader creative effort, he might have taken a place among the major writers of his time. Some acquaintance with the principal themes of his writing, especially as they appear in the texts he wrote for certain of his operas and songs, helps us better to understand and appreciate the nature of his massive achievement in both words and music.

[1] These numbers do not include editions in translation of works originally published in German.

I

Krenek does not believe in the power of music to represent anything. "Any political or extramusical implications which the composer may wish to communicate," he has said, "are conveyed by the words he attaches to his music or to which the music is attached." He has maintained this view since 1918, when he was convinced by Ernst Kurth's book, *Grundlagen des linearen Kontrapunkts,* that music without words is wholly autonomous. If words be used, then it is opera that is "the most efficient medium . . . because the message that may be carried by the words is drastically strengthened by the impact of dramatic action." Or so it would be if anyone but the composer cared seriously about the meaning of an opera. But Krenek has come to think that virtually all the rest—conductors, singers, stage directors, set designers, and audiences—care only for agreeable sounds and dazzling visual effects. His own experiences have tended to confirm this mordant opinion. There was, for example, the uproar surrounding *Sardakai,* the opera he had completed just before delivering the lectures that became these essays. When it was performed in Hamburg later in 1970, the director was so intent upon ideas of his own, which were foreign to the spirit and meaning of the work, that he introduced antithetical elements that created scandal and hostility. Nevertheless, Krenek himself cares so deeply about his meanings and the right words for them that, beginning with *Karl V,* he has regarded the text as paramount, and he changed his working methods to make sure that he himself treated it as such. In those earlier operas for which he had written his own texts, he fashioned words and music simultaneously, which gave him much flexibility. But from *Karl V* onward he first wrote the libretto in full. In fact, the libretto for *Sardakai,* albeit this is a comic opera, took more time and effort than the music, even though the latter is in his complex post-serial style. Given his view of how meanings, including his own, are likely to be treated, one wonders why, apart from his happening to be a talented writer, he attaches such importance to his texts.

For one thing, he is meticulous: he wants things to be done right. Therefore he would take pains over any words of his sent forth into the world. More important, however, is the fact that with few exceptions, notably the magnificent but exceedingly difficult *Lamentatio Jeremiae Prophetae*, his works that use both words and music have been conceived in the hope of affecting an audience—somehow, whether for delight or pity, to move it strongly. This is one reason why the commitment to the twelve-tone technique was a matter of such gravity. He knew well that he was putting formidable obstacles between himself and such general audiences as he had reached before with works like *Jonny spielt auf*. (Later he learned how to manage a style as arcane as serialism in a lighthearted way that helps to make an opera such as *Ausgerechnet und verspielt* [*Computed and Confounded*] appealingly funny.) This hope was a major factor in his turning from the harsh and violent atonalism of a work like the *Second Symphony* to neo-Romanticism and attempting to revitalize traditional forms. Obviously, in works using words, the more clear and powerful they were, the more people he might reach. This became much more important with *Karl V*, for now he passionately wanted to persuade the audience of the value of ancient Austrian traditions and of the peril that threatened them.

He had always been concerned for human rights and dignity. Though his father was an army officer loyal to the emperor (despite a conviction that the government had for long been moving in the wrong direction), Krenek as a young man was imbued with the revolutionary spirit of the times and during his own brief army service at the end of the First World War showed his disaffection by reading Karl Kraus's fiercely antimilitaristic periodical *Die Fackel*, and openly displaying his copies of the heavily censored radical paper *Arbeiter Zeitung*. But though he thought himself a man of the people and strongly approved of the republicanism that followed the collapse of the Hapsburgs, he scorned politics. While a student in Berlin from 1920 to 1923 he had no contact with political activists and was scarcely aware of their existence, despite the temper of that city. His attention was taken up with music and the arts, and his friendships were among those of similar interests. Even so, he admired Mahler for what he took to be a lack of polish—even a deliberate banality—about his music and hoped that by emulating him he could achieve a directness of approach and show his sympathies with the ordinary man.

His first opera, *Zwingburg* (*The Tyrant's Castle*) dealt with the abuse of humble people by a cruel and imperious autocrat. But his next operas, as he points out in the second of these essays, were concerned principally with inward freedom from inhibitions, a matter that was at the moment of much greater personal interest to him. In 1926, after finishing *Jonny spielt auf*, he wrote both words and music for a one-act opera, *Der Diktator*, in which the central figure was modeled on Mussolini. Even so, the treatment was more psychological than political. But two years later he introduced deliberately anti-Fascist implications into his grand opera *Leben des Orest*, for he had begun to worry about the threat of Hitler and his Austrian admirers. Though written in 1929, the song-cycle *Reisebuch aus den Österreichischen Alpen* (*Travelbook from the Austrian Alps*) is suffused with exuberance and hopefulness which were the direct result of Krenek's happiness on returning to his homeland after years abroad. But *Gesänge des Späten Jahres* (*Songs of Later Years*), a cycle written two years later, shows how the concerns latent in the opera had deepened into foreboding and melancholy over the state of his beloved Austria.

Franz Schreker, with whom Krenek studied composing

from 1916 to 1923, had written libretti for his own operas. Regarded by the public as an advanced and daring artist, Schreker belonged heart and soul to the *fin de siècle,* which Krenek's generation was rejecting. His vague, melting dramas were just what would be scorned by a young man who admired Mahler's roughness and felt a kinship with commoners. For his own part Schreker thought Krenek's symphonies much too extreme. Krenek, who had resisted Schreker's musical style, was encouraged in his radicalism by the composer Eduard Erdmann and by Artur Schnabel, remembered today as a concert pianist but at that time himself a composer interested in all the newest tendencies—including jazz, to which he introduced Krenek by way of records and sheet music brought back from tours of America. (This was to prove important to the making of *Jonny spielt auf.*) By the time that Krenek was becoming seriously involved with opera, Schreker's influence even on his music had waned to insignificance, and it appears that Schreker never had much to do with Krenek's development as a librettist and man of letters.

Two others, both remarkable men, did. The first of these was Theodor W. Adorno, later to become a world-renowned sociologist. Krenek met him at the premiere of his second opera, *Der Sprung über den Schatten* (*The Leap over the Shadow*). To Adorno the place of music—especially avant-garde music—was even then a matter of the utmost importance. Slowly they became close friends, working together for the musical journal *Anbruch,* on which Adorno served for a while as the principal editor, and, after Krenek's return to Vienna in 1929, exchanging remarkable letters on the nature of modern music and the role of the composer in contemporary affairs.[2] Adorno was a passionate Hegelian and Marxist who thought that all art, even if it be as abstract as music, must inevitably reflect the social conditions of its time. He certainly did not agree with the aggressively

[2] The letters are to be published by Verlag Suhrkamp.

communistic Hans Eisler, who wrote music to arouse the masses on the grounds that the arts should have direct social utility. But Adorno did believe that the composer could not step outside of history and write solely according to aesthetic considerations. He must have historical awareness, and his music must respond, in keeping with its own true nature, its own idioms and configurations, to the class conflicts of the age.

Adorno was a man of sophisticated intellectual and artistic preferences, and the contemporary music that he most admired—that of Krenek, Schoenberg, Berg, and Webern—was that having the least chance of reaching the ordinary man. He argued, however, that these composers did in fact have the desired historical awareness even when they were alienating themselves. For by remaining faithful to their sense of the direction in which music had to go and refusing to compromise with popular standards of "beauty," they wrote not for art's sake alone, and actually reflected their times, even in their pure music. The very isolation and neglect visited upon them was proof of the deplorable state of society and their own oppression. Adorno hoped that beyond the cataclysm that he saw lying just ahead for mankind there might be a paradisiacal era when avant-garde music would be enjoyed by the ordinary man. Meanwhile, it was an infinitely valuable treasure to be cherished and protected. Krenek agreed that the composer must be aware of and respond to the historical forces impinging upon him and his music, but true to his view that music is autonomous, Krenek believed that the response could be reflected in perceptible ways only in an accompanying text. As a consequence, Adorno was uneasy lest Krenek, despite his commitment to twelve-tone music and the manifest social concern shown in *Karl V* and the essays of this period, might after all be trying to write music for "art's sake"—that is, for the pleasure its beauty would give to an audience.

The second man was the brilliant satirist Karl Kraus, whose periodical, *Die Fackel,* Krenek had read faithfully since his army days. (When he and Willi Reich started *Dreiundzwangzig,* they modeled it on *Die Fackel,* which did not please Kraus.) Though they had had no earlier contact, Krenek came to know Kraus well during the half dozen years before his death in 1936, and to this day he regards Kraus as the strongest influence on his ideas and intellectual development.[3] Kraus was obsessed with the need to maintain the purity of the German language and believed absolutely that careless use of words signified moral laxity. The more imprecise the language, the more corrupt the spirit. His belief made a deep impression on Krenek and certainly encouraged Krenek's own concern for the force and clarity of his texts. Krenek admired, too, Kraus's high moral standards and his flaming indignation, particularly against Viennese journalists and politicians of every persuasion. More than anyone else, Kraus helped him to see the follies of the age and the contrast between man's noble professions and self-serving behavior. He became and remains Krenek's model as a writer and was a "fixed pole" for him during the fearful and chaotic days of Hitler's rise to power. Indeed, Krenek believes that Kraus gave him his vision of man.

But in this he errs, at least in part. There is no gainsaying the effect that Kraus had, but Krenek's view, for all its strong ethical bias, is gentler, more amused, and certainly more magnanimous. In the mid-twenties Krenek had been much attracted by Les Six. It was the moment when he was

[3] This information comes from Krenek himself. Any facts about his life and opinions not derived from his essays, "Self-Analysis," *The New Mexico Quarterly Review,* XXIII (1955), 5–57 (a translation of a booklet entitled *Selbstdarstellung* published in 1948), and "A Composer's Influences," *Perspectives of New Music,* III (1964), 36–41, were furnished to me during conversations with Krenek throughout 1971 and 1972.

most concerned with freedom from inhibitions, and he was charmed by their whimsical manner and their unsolemn belief that music was made from man's delight. He was attracted, too, by their leader, Cocteau, and read all of his works, which he especially enjoyed for their playful tone and lack of pedantry. Now, in his way, Kraus was a consumate actor and could keep a large throng in stitches with the satiric thrusts delivered during his public readings. But everywhere beneath his drollery was a rage against the iniquitous men he saw in places of power and influence—a rage, it almost seemed, against the whole human race for its lazy tolerance of disorder and venality. No such rage burned in Cocteau, who was not less quick to see the follies of mankind. It would be going too far to maintain that he exerted a counterinfluence on Krenek. But there was, and continues to be, in Krenek's temperament something that drew him toward the waggish Frenchman; something that sets him apart from Kraus and helps to account for the gaiety and persiflage of such works as *Ausgerechnet und verspielt* and *Sardakai,* which are a lot closer in tone to French farces than to even the least bitter of Kraus's writings.

II

Thus, under the influence of events and encouraged by Adorno and Kraus, Krenek was undergoing a change in the years just before and after 1930, when he made his decision to remain with music. Turning in disgust from the crude nationalism and vulgarity of the Nazis and their Austrian admirers, he found within himself an allegiance to "the old, universal and supernational empire . . . [a] faith in the idea of an Empire in which all nations had an equitable place."[4] One consequence was that he now desired to play a role in public affairs. And while at first this may have been

[4] "Self-Analysis," p. 27.

a sentimental attachment, it soon became something more profound. Krenek prepared for writing *Karl V* by spending a full year studying the life and times of the emperor during whose reign the traditional values manifested in the universalism of the Holy Roman Empire attained their widest reach, only to disintegrate almost at once into the separatism of the Reformation. By the time he took up the actual writing of his libretto, his allegiance was rooted in historical and doctrinal knowledge. Believing that there was a close analogy between the nationalism that tore Karl's empire apart and that of Hitler, which was dividing Europe into armed camps, Krenek felt that he had to take an active social part. He was showing, in his own way and in keeping with his views of music, the historical awareness that Adorno desired. In order to do what he could without giving up his identity as an artist, he rejoined the Catholic church, which he had left in 1923; he wrote essays and reviews for the *Wiener Zeitung*, the official newspaper of the federal government; he organized concerts of contemporary chamber music; he became a member of a circle of leftist Catholic intellectuals where he met figures high in the political life of Vienna; he publicly supported the government of Dollfuss, even though virtually every other progressive composer regarded it as second-hand, slovenly fascism, and his sympathy for its attemps to resist Hitler by appealing to Austrian patriotic traditions were misunderstood and condemned. He was aware of the authoritarian tendencies of Dollfuss but thought there was no choice but to support him and the Christian Democrats and hope that time would redirect these tendencies.

He was disappointed on all counts. Dollfuss and his successor, Schuschnigg, sought to appease conservatives by adopting a thoroughly reactionary position with respect to the arts. Just when he hoped to reach a larger audience, Krenek found himself increasingly unpopular. (Nothing of his, of course, had been performed in Germany since Hitler's coming to power.) The political nuances of *Karl V* offended the Nazi sympathizers in the orchestra of the Vienna Opera, and the work was withdrawn even though rehearsals had begun.[5] In despair Krenek turned from using texts with any social implications. In 1938 he moved to America and in 1940 wrote a nonpolitical chamber opera, *Tarquin,* which got no attention. It was not until five years later, after he had written much chamber and choral music, that he tried again with *What Price Confidence,* a cleverly plotted little romp for four singers and a piano, which touched upon the old theme of freedom from inhibitions—in about the same way as does Wilde's *The Importance of Being Earnest,* which it somewhat resembles. This was also Krenek's first attempt at writing a libretto in English, which by now he used with facility. Unfortunately, this charming work also did not catch on. Krenek was known as a twelve-tone composer, and Olin Downes had laid down, once and for all, the official line that Americans should have no truck with this eccentric and obsolete technique since they had already surpassed it! In 1950 came *Dark Waters,* a musical melodrama weak in language and characterization, and *The Neighbors,* a little morality play for which Krenek never wrote the music. Meanwhile, throughout the forties he had written exceptionally fine songs and choral works on texts by Kafka, Saint Paul, John Donne, Melville, and Hopkins, among others, doing better with their words than with his own. Not surprisingly, the texts he chose dwelled upon the suffering and loneliness of man in time of war and confusion and his need for assurance of forgiveness and grace.

In 1950 Krenek returned to Europe, and though little remained of the world he had known, his spirits were given a great lift by the eagerness with which brilliant young men,

[5] It had its premiere in Prague in 1938 and its first Austrian performance in Graz in 1969. It has never been performed in Vienna.

who knew and admired his work, came to study with him. (Unfortunately, some of them resented his unwillingness to remain in the role to which they assigned him: important early twelve-tone composer. When he took up electronic music and serialism, their admiration gave way to some not very covert hostility.) Once more he was in touch with the traditions of grand opera, and soon he was at work upon *Pallas Athene weint* (*Pallas Athene Weeps*), his first large-scale opera in nearly twenty years. Though it had a direct pertinence for the United States, where it was written, he used German for his libretto in the expectation that the opera was more likely to be performed in Europe. He was right, for to date it has not been presented in this country, even though it is a magnificent achievement, being the most passionate and profound of his operas. *Karl V* has a grandeur appropriate to the rank of its protagonist and the amplitude of his life, and the exchanges that probe the emperor's motives and the doctrinal implications of his rule and abdication show discernment refined by music of subtle variety and delicate gradations. But for sheer intensity and fully realized meaning, *Pallas Athene weint* surpasses it. Not only is it Krenek's most eloquent treatment of social issues but also the last work to date with any programmatic intention. This is not to suggest that it is propaganda, for it is truly and at all points an integrated work of art. Nevertheless, it quite plainly, if indirectly, speaks for freedom and justice. All the dramatic and musical resources that Krenek could muster are used to show—not to assert, but to *show*—the evil of tyranny and the subversion of loyalties.

Since then Krenek has written another chamber opera in English, *The Bell Tower*; two television operas in German, *Ausgerechnet und verspielt* and *Der Zauberspiegel* (*The Magic Mirror*); a grand opera, also in German, *Der goldene Bock* (*The Golden Ram*); and *Sardakai*, which lies somewhere between a chamber opera and a grand opera.

All may be said to deal in some way with issues of freedom, though in *The Bell Tower* the theme is incidental to a sinister tale about a willful genius who overreaches and destroys himself. All show the infatuations and cupidity of man but none suggests that Krenek has any expectations of making a change in him. Rather, Krenek abides by the views set forth in his second essay that "Musical-dramatic communication will not accomplish any noticeable results in the outside world."[6] All display a wild inventiveness like that to be seen in the third book of *Gulliver's Travels.* But it would be wrong to take Krenek too much at his word and to suppose that they are not, finally, serious, for they are—as *Gulliver's Travels* is serious, though they are not bitter. In them Krenek looks upon mankind with amusement and a charitable but unsentimental affection, and the music enforces this attitude just as it enforced the manifestly solemn and deep concern of *Karl V* and *Pallas Athene weint.* One might say that in the recent operas may be found a nice balance of the spirit of Cocteau with the spirit of Kraus, the tolerant levity of the first and the acute eye for human failings of the second.

III

These, then, are some of the windows through which Krenek has looked upon his time. What has he seen?

In his second essay he remarks, "The idea of freedom . . . has become a dominant concept in many of my dramatic works." He might have added that it is also the theme of a majority of his discursive pieces. But when one surveys the entire corpus, one senses that freedom is but one aspect

[6] He does think, however, that film might be used to treat serious issues. It is a nice irony that much of the uproar over *Sardakai* was initiated by leftist students who plainly disagreed with Krenek. Since the results of their interpretation of the opera were so noticeable, perhaps they, rather than he, had the right of it.

of a more fundamental theme underlying almost everything of importance that he has written; a theme that in fact embodies the principle by which his own imagination has worked with words and tones. It is the relation of a particular element to the larger structure from which it derives whatever identity, meaning, and value it may have: a relation that is dynamic, filled with stress, and, in either the societies or the arts of modern man, precarious and constantly threatening to burst asunder. Which is to say that in our time the relation of the individual to the group is closely analogous to the relation of a tone or similar small unit to the whole composition. What, in such circumstances, is the "freedom" of the individual or of the element in a work of art?

The particular—of whatever kind—may be in and of itself brilliant and exciting to the degree that it is valued for its own sweet sake. But not for long. Man tires of the sensations it generates, however thrilling these may be at first, and looks beyond it to know how it relates, how it matters, to those propositions whereby he tries to understand and direct his experience. In human relations a particular is trivial and meaningless unless it can be seen as part of some larger organization—a society, a culture, a social institution, a ritual, an idea of history—whose human significance is agreed upon by a substantial number of persons. Usually their agreement has been formalized as a dogma and validated by myths, traditions, customs, and the images of man (and of gods or semidivine leaders) which they enclose. But to be effective, validation requires authority, and it is the way of those who have this authority to resist change and suppress variance. Thus the organization that gives the particular its significance is ever in danger of becoming despotic and destroying the particular. The uneasy, ambiguous, and highly problematic relationship between them has evidently always interested Krenek. It is the deep theme of his texts. It is even the relationship that has obtained between himself and his time.

In a musical work much of the interest depends upon the surprise and even momentary dismay or irritation caused by a detail's seeming to oppose the larger structure in which it is contained and the artistic conventions by which the structure is organized. In traditional music a passing tone would be an obvious and commonplace instance of this. But a much greater interest, and with it a pleasure that over-balances our brief discomfort, comes when the opposing detail is understood to have a meaningful place within the structure after all, but having it in ways that we had not foreseen. Ways that actually evolve from and help to redefine the artistic conventions. It is this that brings about the "progress" Krenek refers to in the first of these essays. The startling variation of yesterday becomes a familiar and comfortable part of the conventions of today so that new modes of apparent opposition must be discovered if music is to avoid dullness and banality. But if the opposition goes so far that the sense of the convention (the larger organization) is lost, then every particular is as good as every other particular and no meaning, no cumulative effect, is possible. That is why purely atonal music could not prevail. Why Schoenberg, a conservative at heart, had to return to form. Why, in part, other composers such as Stravinsky took up neoclassicism and Krenek turned to neoromanticism. But neoromanticism could not serve him for long. Its conventions were too well established and familiar, and he quickly used up all ways of relating particulars to them which could give freshness and musical interest.

Yet Krenek knew that if he were to continue with music he would have to have conventions, and so, as we have seen, after long deliberation he turned to the twelve-tone technique. For some time he had thought that the conventions of this technique too closely limited, even predetermined, the music: that they were tyrannical. But careful study of the scores of Schoenberg, Berg, and Webern showed him that much variety within unity was possible, and he could now appreciate the expressiveness and beauty these composers had achieved. In his own composing he learned through experience how to loosen the structures. Adherence to the twelve-tone technique as strict as that in his *Twelve Variations for Piano* and his *Sixth String Quartet* produced, he felt, "too stony a texture to serve as a medium of sufficient flexibility for expression of a reasonably wide range of moods."[7] The same problem, multiplied many times, confronted him when he turned to serialism in 1957. The requirements of action and dialogue made strict serialism in his operas insuperably difficult. Thus, for example, in *Der goldene Bock* serialism guides but does not control the musical relations, though where the libretto permits it, there are passages that are wholly serial. Experience has shown him, moreover, that where serialism determines the selection and arrangement of *all* details, the music becomes so complex that the listener can no longer recognize a theme and its variations and his attention shifts to the particulars as if they were self-sufficient, or as if they were precious objects hovering and glittering in space rather than taking their place in some linear pattern as do the details of earlier music. Paradoxically, the effect of so much organization is a sense of disorder, of there being no organization! In the same way, it is his looser handling of the organization in his recent operas and instrumental works which enables the listener to sense its presence.

The social analogue of the relation of particular to organization and convention—the issue of freedom—is most obvious, and important, in Krenek's two finest operas: *Karl V* and *Pallas Athene weint*. We have seen how the threat of facism and German nationalism turned Krenek into a public

[7] "Self-Analysis," p. 33.

advocate for ancient Austrian traditions and what he interpreted to be the humane universalism of the Holy Roman Empire in the earlier days of Karl's reign. It was no mere coincidence that he simultaneously embraced the twelve-tone technique, with all of its problems concerning the freedom and the expressive relation of a particular musical element to the larger work, and set out to explore the nature of political and religious institutions, with all of their problems concerning the freedom and the relation of an individual to the social organizations whose laws and conventions should give meaning—expression—to his life. Both of these were associated with his return to Catholicism. "I spent much intellectual effort," he wrote later, "on constructing a sort of mystical affinity between the *philosophia perennis* of the Aquinate and the universalism of the dodecaphonic organization. . . . My first work in the newly acquired technique [*Karl V*] was . . . explicitly anti-Nazi, pro-Austrian, and Catholic."[8]

During his year of research on Karl in the archives of the National Library in Vienna he concluded that the real drama was in a discussion of the meaning of the events of Karl's reign rather than in the events themselves. This meant that he could select those episodes that best illustrated the evolution of Karl's own understanding of the relation of the individual to the social organization and the larger significance of even his most private acts and decisions. By means of an ongoing dialectic between Karl and his confessor, Krenek tied the beginnings of the Reformation and the disintegration of the Holy Roman Empire, for which all Europe was the stage, to the torments of conscience in Karl as he tried to answer a question posed by the Voice of God at the beginning of the opera: "Wie hast du das Amt verwaltet? Wie hast du die Aufgabe gelöst?" ("How have you performed your duty? How have you fulfilled your task?").

[8] "A Composer's Influences," p. 39.

It had been all very well for an inhibited European composer to envy and then to emulate a joyously free and instinctual jazz violinist in *Jonny spielt auf*, for the composer was responsible only for himself and had to find what life he could in his own way. But as Karl tells his confessor, "Gott der Herr verlangte von mir, daß ich die Welt im Zeichen Christi einige." ("Our Lord God demanded of me that I unite the world in the sign of Christ.") When he fails, the Turkish sultan sourly observes that the nations of Europe are now free and will use their freedom to exterminate one another. Being unusually conscientious and devout (though in opposition, politically, to the Holy See), Karl could not escape from his enormous burden into a life of impulse and gratification of the senses. In his own person he symbolized the supranational community of Christians. Because it put fealty to God above national interests, that community was not narrowly confining but provided freedom for self-realization along with its restraints, its structures of belief and duty. How *much* freedom was the agonizing issue for the emperor.

As Krenek tells it, Luther, the greatest of Karl's antagonists, had no doubts. On the temporal level man was wholly free, though he was immediately accountable to God for everything he did. He could, if he had faith enough, master and direct events. As a social being he was truly an independent particular, outside of all systems and structures, and infinitely precious in the eye of God, who alone could give meaning and value to his acts. On behalf of such independence of action and conscience, Luther the master tactician made common cause with German nationalists and thereby, in the name of liberty, helped to impose tyranny. When the Jesuit leader, Francisco Borgia, charges Karl on his deathbed with his failure to act against the Germans, Karl replies:

> In jener Zeit kam mir dieser Gedanke, der heut erst zu voller Klarheit reift, und er löst alle Rätsel meiner

> Haltung: Wer handelt, gefährdet den ewigen Ablauf des Ununterbrochenen, und nur das Ununterbrochene hat Sinn. Wer handelt, verfängt sich in Unrecht vor weigen Blicken. Der Weise läßt die Welt den Weg gehn und greift nicht ein. Das ist der Sinn der Herrschaft.
>
> At that time there came to me this thought, which only now becomes mature and clear, and it is the clue to my whole attitude: He who acts endangers the course of the eternal and uninterrupted, and only the uninterrupted has meaning. He who acts entangles himself in evil before the eternal. The wise man lets the world go its way and does not act. That is the character of government.

Rather than endanger the whole upon which all meaning depends, Karl, in the terms of this discussion, refused to function as a particular, which at once opened the way for the destructive particularity of Luther. The two leaders agreed upon the source of all meaning. But one used his belief to withdraw from action, whereas the other used it to plunge into action. Neither, it would appear, understood the right relation of the individual to the larger order. And so, as Karl's life ended in darkness and an overwhelming sense of guilt, Europe, under the forces turned loose by Luther, regressed toward a chaos of wills, ambitions, doctrines, and passions wherein one man, or one nation, acting on self-interest, could enforce an inhumane unity in place of a consensus under a vision of universal equality, love, and brotherhood. Karl had been charged with achieving and preserving that consensus. He failed. Now, Krenek warned by implication, we must not ourselves fail by giving in to the new nationalism. As we know, this implication was not lost upon the pan-Germans of the Vienna Opera in 1934.

Where *Karl V* was written under the threat of Hitler, *Pallas Athene weint* was written under the threat of public hysteria embodied in and exploited by Joseph McCarthy. It depicted the dangers of putting such a high value upon order and structure that the individual was oppressed or destroyed in their name. Laid in Athens during the last phases of the Peloponnesian War, when the traditional Athenian freedom of thought and inquiry was endangered because it was believed that such liberty would weaken the resolve of the people in their struggle with Sparta, the opera shows how the utterly amoral Meletos manipulated the citizens by playing upon their fears to gain power for himself and destroy the free-speaking Sokrates. In an encounter with the totalitarian Agis, king of Sparta, Sokrates puts the issue well:

> AGIS: . . . Ich weiß, was der Welt nottut.
> SOKRATES: So lehre mich, was der Welt nottut.
> AGIS: Ordnung, vor allem Ordnung.
> SOKRATES: Und warum, o Freund, muß Ordnung sein?
> AGIS: Ordnung muß sein, damit Friede sei.
> SOKRATES: Und warum, führst du dann Krieg?
> AGIS: Um Ordnung zu schaffen.
> SOKRATES: Du schaffst nicht Ordnung, nur Gefahr.
> AGIS: Gefahr macht stark.
> SOKRATES: Gefahr schafft Angst.
> AGIS: Wer angst hat, hält Ordnung.
> SOKRATES: Ihm vergeht das Lachen, und du hast Angst vor dem Lachen der Freien. Darum willst du Macht und stiftest Grauen um dich her. Weil du des Menschen Würde verachtest.

> AGIS: . . . I know what the world needs.
> SOKRATES: Then teach me what the world needs.
> AGIS: Order, before all order.
> SOKRATES: And why, oh friend, must there be order?
> AGIS: Order is necessary for peace.
> SOKRATES: Then why do you make war?
> AGIS: To procure order.
> SOKRATES: You do not procure order, only danger.
> AGIS: Danger makes strength.
> SOKRATES: Danger makes fear.
> AGIS: He who is afraid maintains order.

> SOKRATES: Laughter passes from him, and you are afraid of the laughter of the free. That is why you want power and spread terror around you. Because you scorn the dignity of man.

This enrages Agis, and Meletos, quick to seize an advantage, steps forward and ingratiates himself with the conqueror by proposing that Sokrates be first given the pretense of a trial out of consideration for Athenian sensibilities and then executed. Agis agrees, observing that Meletos knows how to deal with the rabble, and Sokrates, who understands perfectly well that he has no chance, goes off to his death. Order—of a kind—has triumphed.

The timely implications of the opera were clear to Krenek's friend, the conductor Dimitri Mitropoulos, who wrote after seeing the libretto,

> Thinking back on the whole situation . . . the interrogation of Socrates which is still left a question today, fills me with dread in front of the present situation of the world and the inability of us intellectuals and thinkers to do more than Socrates did. . . . The answer may lie in artists like you, who are devoting, still with enthusiasm, their skill and their genius to putting in artistic form those great dramas of the human race.[9]

The implications were also plain to those in charge of programming for the government radio station in Prague when they arranged a broadcast of the opera in 1969. The plans were made during the brief period of Dubček's government, though he was out of power by the time the performance took place. This great statement against tyranny seems to have passed unnoticed by the Soviets and their Czech admirers. Again, order—of a kind—had triumphed.

[9] Dimitri Mitropoulos to Ernst Krenek in a letter dated October 10, 1952.

IV

Horizons circled. An "exercise of a late hour" by one who has more than a little claim to be a man of letters. What shall we make of the view from his high perspective?

Let us grant Krenek's assumption that music cannot represent anything and that all conceptual meaning is contained in such language as may be joined with it. Let us for the moment set aside his music (monstrous omission!) and consider only his words. Where do they place him?

It has been remarked of D. H. Lawrence that like Rousseau and Freud he brought about a revolution of sensibility and extended our vision into territories lost in darkness or hidden beyond walls. Writers of his kind are perhaps the most rare. One thinks of only a few others in our time such as Kafka and Proust or on a lower level, perhaps Virginia Woolf and Roethke. Simply to name such writers is to know at once that Krenek is not one of them. It is conceivable that if he had continued to develop in directions hinted at in such early music as his *Second Symphony* or in the subject matter of *Jonny spielt auf* he might have come more nearly to resemble them, though it is inconceivable that he would then have been so affected by Kraus or by the dialectic of Schoenberg's musical history.

No, for all the inwardness of some passages of *Karl V*, for example, he looks outward upon a landscape much surveyed in this century. Which is to say that like many contemporary writers he is concerned with man as a member of a group or striving to become a member: with the identity of the individual in terms of traditions that make possible selfhood in communion, with the meaning of a moment of personal experience in the history of a culture much threatened by disorder. His kinship, therefore, is more with writers like Yeats, Eliot, Mann, and Faulkner. Or, in his attention to the absurd, with writers like John Barth and Beckett.

But the one he most resembles is Joyce, unlike as they are in temperament. Both are acute observers of the human scene with a relish for the ridiculous. Both have a strong sense of historical parallels and use the legends of Greece and their native lands to interpret the present. Both are versed in Catholic doctrine and know well the paradox of man's need for support from such ancient dogmas, coupled with his need to assert and maintain his individuality before them. Both have used that paradox in exploring problems of freedom, order, "progress" in the arts, the artist as seer, the relation of the arts to action. Though seeking to speak through their works on some of the great issues of their age, both have been driven by the momentum of their creativity, and by their refusal to compromise, into using idioms that have alienated them from those they wish to reach. Both have enjoyed the admiration of their fellow artists who, more readily than most, have seen what they were about and could appreciate the effort, integrity, and achievement.

It may seem bold to speak of Krenek with Joyce—until one restores his words to their music. For the music, by its power, variety, suppleness, and congruity, so extends the reach of the words that the comparison is not an impropriety but a way of measuring the scope of Krenek's vision. A wider public now knows and esteems Joyce, and for this the universities deserve much credit. It is to be hoped that the resemblance will hold in this as well, and that Krenek will find the audience he so well deserves, especially in America, which lags behind Europe in performances of the works and honors to the man. In his way he has carried out Adorno's mission for the composer, and if we desire to know more of the meaning of our own late hour when "the unmeasured stands in need of number," we must attend to what he tells us, often in works of surpassing majesty.

It is an auspicious sign that these essays were first offered as lectures in the university which now has the honor to publish them.

Horizon Circled Observed

by WILL OGDON

My report on Ernst Krenek's orchestral composition *Horizon Circled* attempts the futile task of describing a musical work still unexperienced by most of its readers. The author, as observer of *Horizon Circled,* can only hope that these readers will share some of the pleasure, edification, and excitement he gained from his study of the score and its tape-recorded performance by a European orchestra conducted by the composer.

This observer can only agree with the widely held opinion that nothing replaces the musical experience: The music must communicate everything essential to its own understanding. Words attempting to describe its events are too often superfluous or even misleading. But he also believes that something must be done to counteract the insiduous vacuum of our time in which a *Horizon Circled* languishes relatively unheard: our very future is being cheated of its musical heritage.

Horizon Circled, like other significant musical statements of our time, is too rarely heard in concert and, as yet, is unrecorded for public consumption. Even its score is still unavailable for study except to conductors willing to brave the hostile apathy that continues to devitalize our musical culture. There would seem to be too few of these in responsible positions of leadership to effect any meaningful change in our condition.

But *Horizon Circled* does exist—it is being heard and its signs are being studied. *Horizon Circled* can be easily recognized as the gift of a man of intellect and wisdom, an eminent composer rich in technique and experience, one able to communicate with his fellow men.

Those of us ready to receive such a gift must be willing to demand the fruits of our heritage. Perhaps others, by accumulating new and diverse musical experiences, will ripen their ability to accept such gifts. Unless this happens, the fate of music as a vital sign of our culture will continue to hang in the balance.

Horizon Circled was commissioned, and first performed, by the Meadow Brook Festival of Rochester, Michigan. Its composition was begun in Vienna on the first of January 1967 and completed in Baltimore on February 20 of that same year.

Horizon Circled is scored for a sympthony orchestra of doubled winds with bass clarinet; for four horns and doubled trumpet and trombone with tuba; for timpani, vibraphone, xylophone, harp and piano; for an orchestral body of strings and an imposing array of percussion. It is cataloged as the composer's opus 196 and is available for performance from Barenreiter Verlag of Kassel, Basel, London, and New York.

I

Horizon Circled is more than the sum of its six movements Azimuth, Elevation, Meridian, Inner Circle, Parabola, and Zenith. It is also a well-integrated symphonic structure, its separate parts being interconnected in a complex but most coherent manner. We will support this claim by reproducing the diagram that Krenek himself sketched for his lecture audience at the University of California at San Diego in La Jolla in February of 1970 (fig. 6).

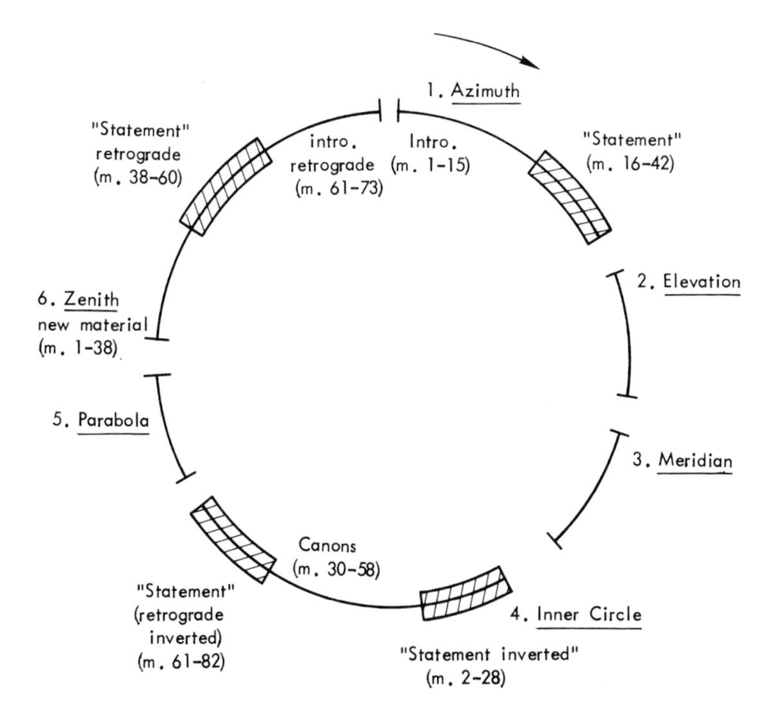

Krenek's diagram makes clear the composition's broad structural interconnections primarily attained by varied recurrences of a twenty-measure thematic section first stated immediately after its introduction. The diagram also points out the arch to which the final retrograde statement of that theme contributes, an arch that returns the listener to the composition's beginning, after having traveled from its first movement, Azimuth, through its last, Zenith (from A to Z). But Krenek's schematic was not meant to reveal the complex interlacing of motivic detail which makes *Horizon Circled* texturally and structurally symphonic.

A study of the structural integration of *Horizon Circled* can be fascinating as can a study of its textural and timbral variety. Few compositions scored for the conventional symphony orchestra have equaled the rich diversity of textures and timbres exhibited in *Horizon Circled,* at least not within the tighter thematic confines of a symphonic structure.

As the overall flavor of Krenek's huge output of the last fifty years is recalled, how characteristic this dual condition seems. Krenek's work has always displayed on the one hand, a colorfully varied palette and, on the other, its close attention to detailed relationships. The synthesis of these two polarities might well represent the musical model of the composer's philosophical dialectic on freedom and responsibility. At any rate, the synthesis proves to be an aurally satisfying one in *Horizon Circled.*

Its second aspect is related to the motive-working tradition epitomized by the late Beethoven quartets. But how remarkable to find the forming of *Horizon Circled* so motivically and even thematically oriented after Krenek's previous decade of exploration into the unmapped structural territory demanded by total serialism.

But of course! If these adventures of the later 1950s and 1960s, coming after Krenek's motivically structured twelve-tone music, could have investigated modes of unpredictable structuring, then surely Krenek's more recent study of Anton Webern's sketchbooks could have reengaged his always lively mind with the still vital potential of the motive.

II

Horizon Circled begins in exuberant fashion. A fortissimo blow of "hammer on wood" sharpens the attack of the pianist's murderous karati chop to the lower strings of the piano. That rude blow sets off the shrillest howls of upper winds and brass, their beginnings made razor sharp by a FFF tremolo, on "all strings behind the bridge," played by the entire string section. Simultaneously, the low brass and winds growl their lowest tones as loudly as possible, aided by the timpanum's low E and abetted by the pianist who crashes right and left forearms at the same time to the high and low registers of his keyboard.

A subito drop to pianissimo only presages an inexorable crescendo in both winds and brass that drills to his seat the listener already jolted by the savagery of this unforwarned attack on ears and nerves. Gradually, he is allowed to regain his more typical composure during a still highly energized but less concentrated wind and brass passage whose texture is made up of separately timed but coexisting twelve-tone groups. Their declining volume is counteracted by an unrelenting crescendo on field drum and glissandoing timpanum, joined a few seconds later by the scream of the string section's highest and lowest pitches (fig 7).

Again, repeated and even-noted, twelve-tone groups unroll but this time in the better mannered strings which gradually adjust themselves to a unifying tempo. Their multiproportioned writhing within a narrow pitch band is joined by a rapidly repeating harp configuration. This high, tinkling harp figure then accompanies a short, scurrying sequence of woodwinds from high to low followed by a rather lengthy but seemingly exhausted muttering in the brass. And so *Horizon Circled* is flung into orbit.

III

These several muttering measures have concluded an aggressive introduction of almost chaotic character. Their static quality seems curiously appropriate at this point, perhaps like the troubled calm after a violent natural event. The immobile aspect of these measures results from a fixed

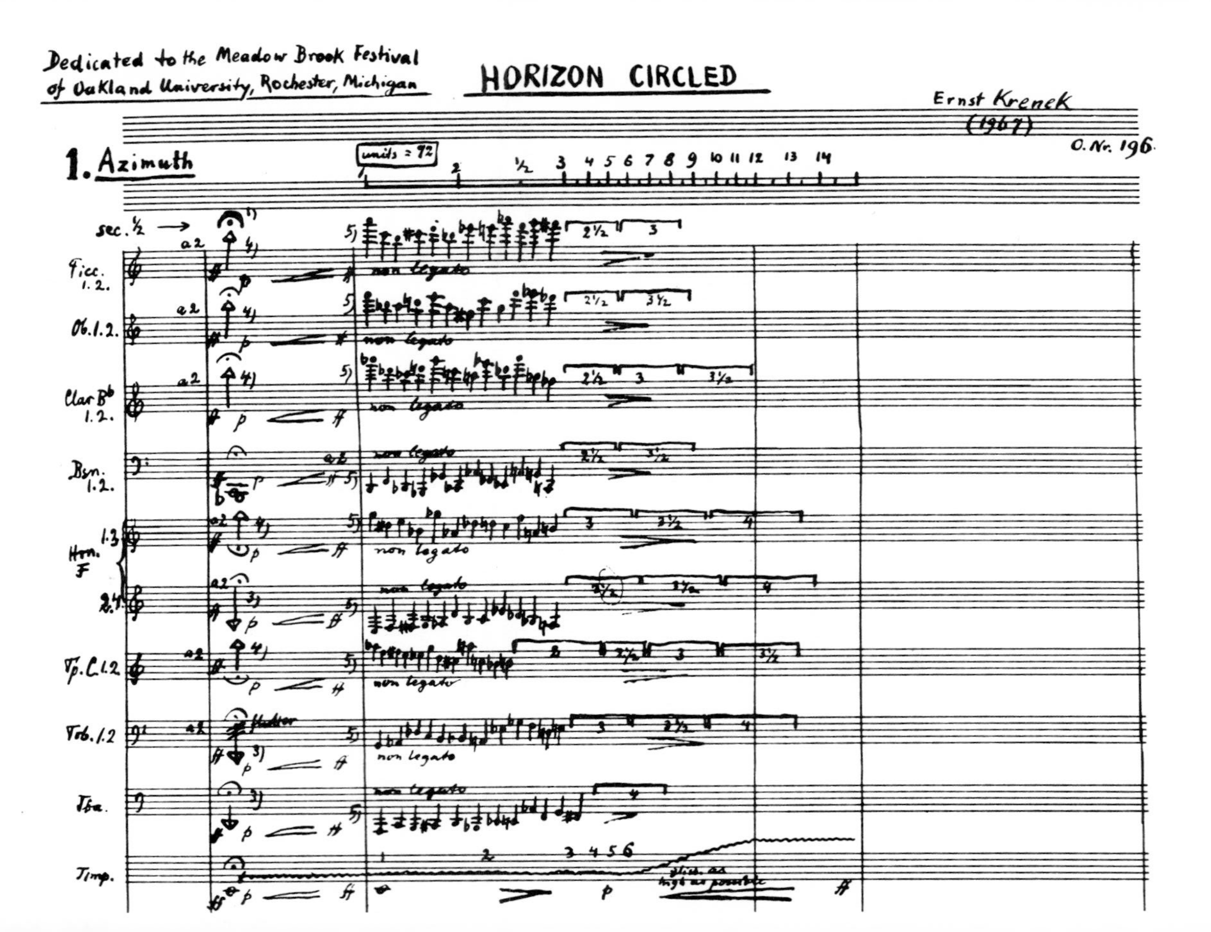

Dedicated to the Meadow Brook Festival
of Oakland University, Rochester, Michigan
HORIZON CIRCLED
Ernst Krenek
(1967)
O. Nr. 196.
1. Azimuth
units = 92
sec. ½ →
Picc. 1.2.
Ob. 1.2.
Clar B♭ 1.2.
Bsn. 1.2.
Hrn. F 1.3
2.4
Tp. C. 1.2
Trb. 1.2
Tba.
Timp.
a2
non legato
flutter
gliss. as high as possible

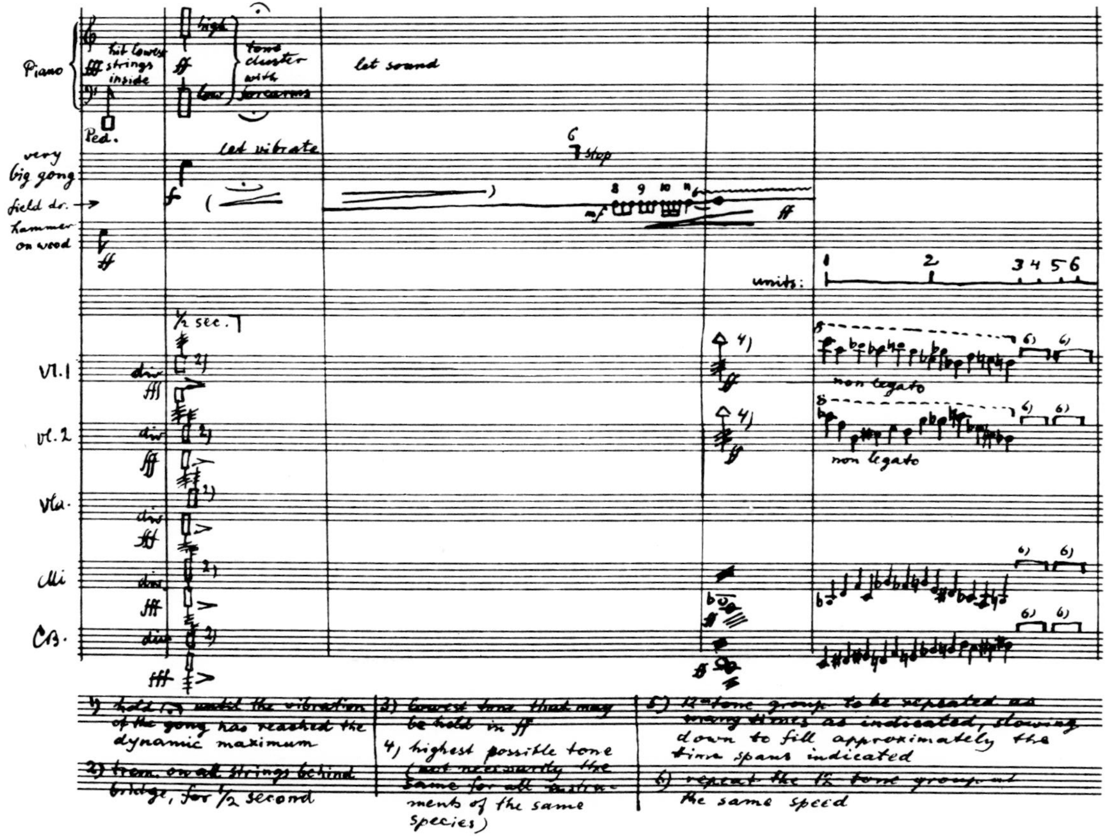

Piano — hit lowest strings inside — Ped. — high / low — tone cluster with forearms — let sound

very big gong — let vibrate — 6 stop

field dr. → 8 9 10 11 — mf — ff

hammer on wood — ff

units: 1 2 3 4 5 6

½ sec.

Vl. 1 — div. — fff — non legato

Vl. 2 — div. — fff — non legato

Vla. — div. — fff

Vc. — div. — fff

Cb. — div. — fff

1) hold until the vibration of the gong has reached the dynamic maximum

2) trem. on all strings behind bridge, for ½ second

3) lowest tone that may be held in ff

4) highest possible tone (not necessarily the same for all instruments of the same species)

5) 12-tone group to be repeated as many times as indicated, slowing down to fill approximately the time spans indicated

6) repeat the 12-tone group at the same speed

registral identification with this limited amount of pitch material (fig. 8).

B flat is always in the muted first horn and always on third line, treble clef. C is always played by muted trumpet and is invariably middle C. There are no exceptions to the fixed pitch/timbre condition of this passage and its unchanging piano dynamic only confirms its immobile quality. But the melodic elements of these six measures are neither fixed nor unchanging. A forward developing pitch line is defined by the top notes of intervals and chords as well as by unaccompanied, single tones. An unsymmetrically permutated pattern of durations also helps invest the tonal material with some sense of forward propulsion.

Which relative condition—a stasis or kinesis—seems dominant becomes a subjective listening decision. Since the passage is for brass choir, the related tone colors help convey an impression of sameness. But if the first horn or muted trumpet were not so strictly confined to treble B flat or to middle C, the character of the passage would be quite different.

We are still prepared to follow a melodic line played on the same instrument rather than divided among several. It is very easy, then, for an inexperienced listener to pay attention to the registrally exposed horn as it persistently repeats its given pitch. Whether or not that same listener can follow Krenek's elastically shaped line, formed on a three-octave span of quickly varied brass timbres, is perhaps more questionable. Yet, both active and static qualities are concurrently present in this passage and their presence is responsible for a curious impression of restless calm.

IV

The permutated continuity of the six-measure passage just described is snipped off by a quick, three-note, trumpet figure. These preceding measures have done their structural duty: they have functioned as a bridge to Azimuth proper, the first movement of *Horizon Circled.*·

Why Azimuth? Does its character, texture, or structure suggest something related to mathematics or astronomy? Or perhaps Krenek intends his listeners to be prompted by titles into some mood similar to that conjured up by the film *2001*?

The rhythmic precision and textural economy of Azimuth more readily suggest the activity of measuring than some mystical traversing of the heavens. And, after *Horizon Circled*'s introduction, there would not seem to be anything very dramatic left to say at the moment.

Azimuth is spare and it is easy to hear as a series of phrases. How often these phrases seem snipped off by the three-note trumpet motive already mentioned. The opening period of two phrases is neatly balanced and, after that first period, all succeeding phrases begin with an expressive motive in the strings, a motive readily identified not only by its string timbre but by its rhythmic pattern and pitch contour as well.

On reflection, Azimuth seems as expository within its context of *Horizon Circled* as do statements of a first and second theme within the exposition of a sonata movement. It is even rounded off by a few closing measures of bassoon melody, not so much in the transitioning manner of connected Lisztian movements but more conclusively like the double bar approach of an earlier binary form.

But as these assertions are reread, it becomes apparent how much this observer has written his own proclivities into Krenek's music. The trumpet's three notes that cut off the transitional measures, from introduction to Azimuth proper, are also the first notes of the twenty-measure statement that Krenek will repeat three times: first inverted, then reversed and inverted and, finally, backward.

Perhaps the phrase structure of Azimuth is not so clear after all—especially if one can be allowed to interpret its beginning motive as an ending! One thing appears fairly certain, however—and it has been noticed before by this admirer—Krenek has made a virtue of structural ambivalence, although continuity does seem served more than articulalation and form does seem to grow or unwind more than it stops and starts.

An aesthetic value resides, then, is *not* being able to

so easily and exactly parse the structure of *Horizon Circled*. This built-in modicum of mysterious ambivalence might enhance *Horizon Circled*'s aural effect, but it also allows interpreters of both the performing and analyzing variety to go astray or to find themselves asserting their own prejudices and, more often than not, placing their feet solidly in their mouths.

V

An interplay between looser and tighter modes of time control is active on two fronts in *Horizon Circled*. Its time dialectic functions structurally when a more exact notation of musical time is apposed to time material which is more loosely notated. The dialectic also functions texturally when one layer of music, strictly notated, is superimposed upon another whose time relationships are less strictly coordinated.

Krenek's structural relating of looser and tighter time structures is somewhat analogous to the principle of open and closed forms as used from the later eighteenth century through, at least, Arnold Schoenberg. The Beethoven sonata movement, for example, delineated its thematic statements from introductions, transitions, and developments by linking more to less balanced phrase structures. In *Horizon Circled*'s introduction, for example, a loosely timed coexistence of instruments is followed by a gradual gearing-up to a given tempo and then by a carefully measured and conventionally notated conclusion.

In the fourth movement (which Krenek has named Inner Circle) larger sections, conventionally timed and notated, are separated by coloristic flurries that are not measured but can only be cued in and out by the conductor.

One movement of *Horizon Circled* which uses its deviation from conventional time notation for other than traditional functions is the fifth, Parabola. Here, Krenek expresses a rubato relationship to an underlying time pulse by positioning the notation of instrumental melodies physically around the measure's beat but foregoing any rationally counted subdivision.

Horizon Circled's second movement, Elevation, offers a clear example of textural juxtaposing of looser and tighter time structures. Elevation's introduction is a series of measures into which notated material is loosely fit by all members of the string section. The lines are more individually sensed than counted and there is no particular attempt on the part of the composer to control proportional time relationships. These lines are repeated as an ostinato but they are only loosely coordinated with each other and with the conventionally timed-notated melodic material unfolding in the wind and brass. This double layering of exactly and inexactly timed musics seems readily comprehensible and their aural synthesis produces a fresh and telling aesthetic experience.

VI

Horizon Circled's second movement, whose introduction we have been describing, is especially intriguing as a form. Krenek has followed the expository Azimuth with a short movement that is casually but inexorably organized as a series of sections linked together with hardly any motivic cross reference. The impression of casualness proves deceptive, however. As the tempo shifts gears and as the piece tightens and then hurtles to its end, one realizes that Elevation is all of a piece in spite of sharply contrasted sections.

The deception is partly inherent in the unifying role played by the strings which undergird the thematic surface of the principal section of this movement, in winds and brass, with ostinato material first exposed in the four-measure introduction. The strings sound wayward and unfocused while brass and wind instruments present unhurried and easily followed statements and imitations of a few motivic shapes.

This section is divided into its two parts by a sudden and loud, brass and percussion announcement of two measures. The strings could hardly care less: they buzz hazily along, each not attempting to adjust bowing or tempo to that of his neighbor.

Following this thematic section, the violins (divided into six parts and playing harmonics), along with a solo cello, float upward into their stratospheric range where they balance precariously, fading from view, part by part. At the same time, the violas and divided basses are quietly sinking down to tremble in their lower ranges as a brisk but quiet percussion canon begins.

Since the double basses continue to pulsate on their lowest E and F during this percussion passage (immediately followed by a brilliant fall orchestra cadenza thrown from group to group but with minimal participation of the strings), and since the movement's closing stretta, following on the heels of the cadenza, is only in the strings (martellato and in four part imitation), one becomes aware of how unifying a role the strings have really played and how much they have dominated the character and structure of Elevation.

VII

Did Krenek remember Josquin's complex mensuration canons when he composed this intricate percussion passage? Josquin's canonic lines start from time base O and proceed at different rates of speed proportionally calculated. After four introductory measures, so does this percussion canon of Krenek's. But unlike the Josquin (or other typical canons), the statistical content from part to part is not the same. Four layers of similar, yet statistically different patterns of drum tattoos are exactly repeated except for the time spans that separate their repetitions (fig. 9).

In the introductory measures the field drum establishes both its own pattern of three sixteenth notes and the duration of the duple measure in which this passage is cast. In successive measures, three other patterns are introduced: first a quintuplet, then a seven-element pattern subdividing

the basic quarter note into six parts, and then a nine-element pattern that subdivides the quarter into seven.

After the fifth measure, an arithmetic contracting and expanding of the interstitial rests begin to shift the coincidence of the four patterns. Translated into numbers, and beginning with measure five, this arithmetic contraction or expansion of pattern and rest (considered as a unit) adds up to the following numbers of pulse durations (remembering that the pulsations of the four parts are not moving at the same rate of speed):

Part 1: 7/8/9/10/10/9/8
Part 2: 13/12/11/10/9/8/7
Part 3: 14/14/13/12/11/10/9
Part 4: 19/18/17/16/15/14/13

The reader will observe in the scored example just how this time-shifting relationship musically coordinates the four time patterns. He will also notice how successive units (considering each unit as a single presentation of all four patterns) overlap, or do not overlap in one case.

Krenek's mensuration canon is an engrossing listening experience, its dry, mechanistic character having been somewhat ameliorated by changing the timbre of the repeating septuplets from wood block to timpanum rim to choked cymbal.

VIII

This twelve measure percussion episode, so precisely time-computed, seems rigidly unchanging when compared to the glittering cadenza that immediately follows. The resonant "ring and clang" of the cadenza's succeeding blocks of sound seems almost gamelan-like in quality (especially the timbral block made up of piano, harp, vibraphone, and xylophone) and a resonantly live hall will handsomely amplify Krenek's sonorous effects in this section.

First the woodwinds, then the keyboard and mallet instruments with harp, then a remarkable col legno battuto in all the strings overlapped by a short brass flourish. Again the winds are followed by the keyboard, harp, and mallet instrument configuration (this time in clusters and glissandi), succeeded by a parallel to the col legno strings as wind and brass rattle valves and keys. Each timbre is to be played as fast as possible. The resonantal decay of these timbre blocks are controlled by directing the conductor to cue successive orchestral groups according to a time design formed of a varying number of clock-time units in seconds.

IX

The crackling stretta and cadence that hurtles Elevation to its close clears the air for a sultry, lethargic movement called Meridian. An impression of a scherzo movement followed by a ruminating and lyric adagio is unmistakable. Meridian's thick-textured opening, first in the brass and then joined by bassoons and flutes, prepares and underlays a rather curious piano phrase which seems to hum a fragment of some nostalgic tune from a half-forgotten past.

The piano is answered by a nonchalant, almost careless, solo violin, its two-note phrase fragments sung over the same harmonic accompaniment now in woodwinds and the horns. This second phrase is rather brusquely closed off by a staccato piano figure but the languor of the music still hangs in the air because of a sensitive harp doubling of the piano's last note and because open piano strings (the pianist is instructed to silently depress certain lower keys) are sympathetically resonated by the harmonic frame of the staccato cadence.

The closing phrase of Meridian's opening section begins with a sensuous melodic phrase in the clarinet after which remaining measures spin out a series of two- and three-note motives (largely stepwise) on various instruments. Their lack of energy seems to emphasize the tropical turgidity of Meridian's atmosphere.

The composer is aware of the implications of his title on more than one level. Krenek associates his music with the meridional south. His depiction of physical warmth is translated into emotional warmth so that Meridian seems to convey not only a climatic atmosphere but a highly charged emotional one as well.

We are not surprised to find Meridian's middle section developing a large-scale, lyric line in the strings, aria-like in phrase and contour, and reaching over its length of twenty-eight measures, a passionate climax. This culmination is elided with the phrase that opens Meridian's final section, a phrase that recalls the movement's opening bars. This new phrase, once again largely in brass with winds, also allows an emotional subsidence and transfers the listener back to the more neutral atmosphere of Meridian's beginning. After its lethargic character has been reestablished and following the reminiscence of the solo violin, the movement ends with a repetition of that nostalgic piano tune.

X

It seems useful to point out at this time the broader implications of specific technical details found in Meridian and in other movements of *Horizon Circled* as well. One of these has to do with Krenek's general predisposition to disregard or minimize meter in its more traditional sense. These measure bars do not carry, a priori, their expected baggage of weak and strong beats. Rather, the measure is considered as so much musical space to be filled and Krenek's melodic material, such as that in the aria section of Meridian, fills it as it must, maintaining its own motivic stresses regardless of where they fall within the bar.

One cannot with impunity, then, read into Krenek's scores syncopes and metrical plays and balances such as those encountered in some of the later music of Anton Webern. But Krenek is careful to reduce the possibility of metrical confusion or misunderstanding in his scores by supplying agogic and dynamic accents along with slurs and staccato markings that help define the shape of motives and melodic lines. The result of Krenek's metrical prose allows a more relaxed and time-floating environment for those contrapuntal elements of his textures which are not geared to a preset, metrical plan.

Textural pitch placement, commented on before in our discussion of Azimuth, functions once again in the opening section of Meridian. A harmonic layering of pitches is formed in its first phrase and then quite consistently adhered to during the course of the section. Its note returnings often identify specific harmonic and melodic aggregates. This technique of registrally fixing pitch elements within a harmonic texture contributes to the peculiar atmosphere of Meridian which this observer has interpreted as lethargic and sensuous.

XI

A noteworthy coincidence should be mentioned while we are still in the vicinity of Meridian. The coincidence has to do with the wispy piano fragment heard in this movement's opening and concluding phrases. This evocative little tune calls to mind a very similar melody found in Krenek's Symphonic Elegy composed more than twenty years before *Horizon Circled* (figs. 10*a*, *b*).

The coincidence raises interesting questions of hidden associative meanings, especially since the *Elegy* of 1946 was a heartfelt response to news of the tragic death of Anton Webern, and since the music of Meridian demonstrates so pictorially and expressively an affinity with its title. Only the composer will (or need) know answers to such questions, unless there is ample evidence of other similarities, of course. This observer, with some trepidation about being indelicately nosey, put the question to the composer both about these examples in particular and about Krenek's possible use of mottoes with associated meanings in general.

No, Krenek was unaware of the similarity between the two melodic fragments. Yes, it was unconscious and unpremeditated: He had in mind, while writing Meridian's piano tune, some feeling of melancholy, some nostalgic feeling. Since this observer's description was written prior to his conversation with the composer, perhaps one should offer this as another piece of evidence supporting music's ability to convey feeling. But no, he had never consciously written motives or other materials which for him carried secret, associated meanings.

Although the question was not asked because its answer appeared obvious, we should add that Krenek has not avoided musical illustration. Obviously, an opera composer develops all sorts of verbal underlinings. And, obviously, the composer has matched the character of *Horizon Circled* to the titles of these individual pieces we have been describing.

But a motto or musical fragment that acts as a leitmotiv within a purely instrumental piece such as *Horizon Circled* does not seem to be any premeditated part of Krenek's compositional technique. His replies during our telephone conversation, however, always allowed or even expected, that such hidden allusions might exist without the composer having to consciously manufacture them.

XII

The gamelan-like flourish described in our discussion of Elevation's cadenza is resorted to once again in Inner Circle, the fourth movement of *Horizon Circled,* where it functions not as a cadenza but as a separating device. These ringing announcements are wonderfully stylish in this several-sectioned movement whose long, middle section is a complicated series of canons.

But, personally, I find the opening section of the final movement, Zenith, to be the most aurally arresting. At one point, the texture of this thirty measure section is formed from twenty string parts, all tremolo. Glissandi surge through the near total range of the strings, punctuated by short barks and growls in wind and brass and sounding something like Stravinsky.

This pyrotechnical display of gliding string tremolos is easy for this observer to associate with the heavens for he remembers that Krenek used a somewhat similar device once before to represent the northern lights. The effect of blocked string tremolandi occur twice in his impressive setting of Herman Melville war poems composed for orchestra and womens' voices and called *Cantata for War Time.*

Zenith's opening section is superseded by the jerking immobility of a piano vamp that then underlays a surprising episode of scattered, whistling glissandi, sul ponticello—something like a compressed, time-film of meteorites and comets by Walt Disney.

It is at this point that *Horizon Circled* retraces its first steps, Azimuth's twenty measure theme in backward motion followed by a retrograde presentation of the entire introduction. And it is here that this observer of *Horizon Circled* feels compelled to cease his comments on its delights and marvels.

There is much left to remark upon and to compare, such as the broad diversity of textures that reshape and enliven the progress of the work, or the many subtle touches of orchestration that could easily form a compendium of instruction in that particular technical discipline. The composer, himself, has commented elsewhere in this book on the time and texture influence that serialism exerted on *Horizon Circled*'s fifth movement, Parabola.

But the author is reminded that hearing music rather than reading descriptions is the straight and narrow way to musical salvation. The reader desiring a more satisfying, personal conversion is advised to look for that rare concert or for that improbable recorded performance of *Horizon Circled*. When discovered, the immediacy and strength of the listening experience will surely render these words by comparison obsolete and ineffective.

ERNST KRENEK AT THE UCSD CAMPUS

Krenek with author John Stewart, provost of John Muir College.

Krenek with composer Roger Reynolds. *(Harry W. Crosby)*

Krenek with composer Robert Erickson; Gladys Krenek in the background. *(Harry W. Crosby)*

Krenek with philosopher Herbert Marcuse in the Mandeville Suite. *(Harry W. Crosby)*

Krenek at the piano; Beverly Ogdon in the background. *(Harry W. Crosby)*

Krenek with faculty members in the electronic studio; from left, James Campbell, Thomas Nee, John Silber. (*Harry W. Crosby*)

Krenek lecturing. *(Glasheen Graphics)*

*Minutes of a Conversation between Will Ogdon and Ernst Krenek**

(While visiting at the UCSD campus, Ernst Krenek once in a while took the opportunity to touch in more informal conversation upon some subjects that attracted his attention as he was circling his horizon.)

WO: I am always a bit curious when I think of you living out in the desert, Ernst. Why did you settle in Palm Springs and when?

EK: In 1966. After having lived in the Los Angeles area for nearly twenty years, I moved to the desert which I had always contemplated longingly ever since I saw it for the first time when I came to this country, in 1938.

WO: Do you miss Los Angeles?

EK: Once in a while I feel some nostalgia for the colorful animation of the Sunset Strip, the Miracle Mile, the excitement of a place that looks like an exhibition to be torn

* Will Ogden, "Conversation Will Ogdon with Ernst Krenek," *Perspectives of New Music*, copyright 1972 by Princeton University Press. Reprinted by permission of Princeton University Press.

down tomorrow and to be built up again after some new mod fashion.

WO: But what about the artistic and intellectual stimuli of a large city?

EK: Since most of what was demanded of me in L.A. was to function as a taxpayer and consumer of groceries and gasoline, I thought I might exercise these functions just as well at a place where landscape and climate were more congenial. For the rest, I visit L.A. quite frequently, mainly to keep abreast of the movies.

WO: If you are a "movie bug" why is it you haven't written a score for film?

EK: I have never been asked to—and that may be just as well, considering the way music has been treated there. But I feel that the film has become more and more the only medium for dealing seriously with the problems of our time.

WO: That is a surprising statement from a composer of about twenty operas—and some of them commenting on contemporary attitudes and problems.

EK: In my operas I have always taken the subject matter very seriously, and I have tried to convey some definite ideas by the words that I set to music.

WO: Most of your operas have been set to your own librettos have they not?

EK: Nearly all of them. The most notable exception is my *Orpheus and Eurydice*, written in 1923 after a play by the Austrian painter Oskar Kokoschka.

WO: Do you write the play first? And how aware of the music are you while working on the play and vice versa?

EK: Working on my earlier operas, I started sketching the music when I had completed a definite and elaborate scenario in which the progress of the plot was outlined in detail. The actual dialogue originated together with the music. This method had the advantage of being very flexible. I could expand or condense certain passages according to what the musical development seemed to require, modify expressive emphasis, and the like.

WO: Have you abandoned this method of working in later operas?

EK: When I began to work on *Charles V* about 1930 I decided to complete the libretto before giving definite shape to the musical ideas of the project. I have applied this procedure ever since.

WO: This would seem to limit flexibility, something you considered an advantage prior to *Charles V*. Why did you decide to forgo that advantage?

EK: I think it was the weight and significance of the subject matter that made me feel that the statements of the libretto should be formulated very carefully so that they would live up to higher literary standards than those traditionally applied to so-called lyrics. Consequently, I worked much longer on the librettos and made fewer changes when I eventually set them to music.

WO: Specifically, what subject matter did you consider so important?

EK: While in my early operas I was mainly concerned with the idea of social freedom from oppression and personal freedom from inhibitions, I gradually became conscious of the factor of accountability, and in *Charles V* the concept of justification is the hinge on which the play revolves. The Renaissance emperor reviews the various stages of his life in an attempt to justify his abdication, his giving away his powers of action. The strong emphasis on Christian universality made this opera utterly intolerable to the Nazis, a fact that contributed to my emigration from Europe. Political overtones are also very strong in *Pallas Athene Weeps,* which I wrote in America in 1954. The destruction of the Athenian democracy at the hands of the Spartan tyrants was a metaphor easily to be interpreted in terms of situations of our own experience. Through my preoccupation with serial music I became more and more intrigued with the philosophical problems of time and space. Witness the *Golden Ram,* written in the early sixties—a playful and sinister paraphrase of the ancient Greek legend of the Argonauts and the Golden Fleece, spanning thousands of years and two continents.

WO: If you found your "serious operas" capable of considering such important ideas, why do you now feel that the film might be a better medium for dealing with serious subject matter?

EK: Only much later I became aware of having, in *Charles V,* applied some dramaturgical devices that suggest techniques more germane to moving pictures than to the stage, such as for instance splitting the place of the action, rapid changes of locale, flashbacks, and the like. The inclination to use such devices consciously became more pronounced in my later operas. The flight of the Golden Ram over the Atlantic and his landing among the Navajos in our own time, the journey of the ship *Argo* through the clashing rocks of the Symplegades, the transformation of a dragon into the Indian princess Medea—these and many other details very loudly call for filmic treatment. Therefore, I welcomed the opportunity of writing two operas for European TV. In one of them, *The Magic Mirror,* I am again playing with the mystery of time, as the action switches from ancient China to modern Europe. The other TV opera treats the dialectical relationship of predetermination and chance—as it was hammered into my consciousness through the preoccupation with serialism—in a whimsical vein, illustrating it as a contest between computer and roulette. Thus it turned out that the more seriously I seemed to take opera, the more I felt a gnawing suspicion that opera was basically an absurd medium, best suited to self-irony. I remembered how many opera fans were cheerfully declaring that they did not care at all whether the happenings on stage made any sense, and I came to the conclusion that the only person that took the libretto seriously was the composer.

WO: What did you find particularly interesting about working in the medium of television?

EK: Apart from those things mentioned earlier, it is the possibility of focusing the attention of the viewer onto any detail I wish to bring to his attention, the possibility of juxtaposing events far distant from each other in time and space, and of obtaining maximum intelligibility of the words by careful recording and judicious final mixing of the audio channels. You see I am still attaching some importance to the text.

WO: And you haven't been attracted to improvisatory or extemporaneous music theater?

EK: As a matter of principle I have no inhibition against any experimentation of this kind, be it ever so "bold" or antiestablishmentarian. Perhaps my experience with these manifestations is too limited for permitting me to utter relevant opinions about them. My essential misgivings are based on the fact that most of these "happenings" failed to be as exciting as they were announced to be.

WO: You have attended, then, certain extemporaneous performances or happenings?

EK: I have witnessed some of the musical "games" recently *en vogue*, where the participants or participant groups try to "snatch" given musical material from each other, to finish faster, or the like. But since, when confronted with competitive games, I share the attitude of the shah of Persia who, when invited by the Austrian emperor to watch the horse races, replied, "Thank you very kindly, your Majesty, but I know that some horses run faster than others, and which ones, I don't care," I am unable to get excited about who wins such a game. All that interests me is what I hear, and that is frequently disappointing. Witnessing similar activities, I gain the impression that it is perhaps great fun to partake of them, as for instance in a jam session, but to listen to the sounds resulting from such parlor games is usually much less entertaining. And when the mixed-media show includes the audience in the name of participatory something or other, I am not very cooperative. I have always enjoyed getting mixed up with actors, and especially actresses, but rather backstage than in the aisles.

WO: But your own recent work has involved chance, has it not?

EK: That is correct. I have become fascinated with the interrelation of predetermination and chance ever since I entered the province of serialism. What interested me there was the unpredictability of certain parameters as necessitated by the total preorganization of others. This I feel to be different from chance as a result of hazard, such as tossing coins or rolling dice. I was excited dealing with the surprises that a nearly totally predetermined musical process would produce, excited by musical results that I probably would never have obtained had I not set up the serial machinery.

WO: Certain recent works of yours offer optional routes to performers and various less controlled textural results to listeners, do they not?

EK: There are two ways in which I deliberately opened the door to unpremeditated sound combinations. In two or three orchestral works (e.g., *Horizon Circled),* I wrote movements in which the basic twelve-tone set is played in each of the consecutive time segments, while the location of the individual tones within each segment is not precisely determined, only relative positions are indicated so that the players have some leeway in sounding their tones. The purpose of this arrangement is to impart to the music a floating, unstable, and "unsquare" character.

Another step forward in indeterminacy has to do with the concept of the mobile. In my orchestra piece *From Three Make Seven* I composed two blocks of music that may be combined and synchronized in countless different ways.

A similar idea is the basis of my *Fibonacci Mobile.* Here again the shorter (faster) and longer (slower) elements may be combined in many different ways.

WO: Isn't all this a demonstration of progressive ways of writing variations?

EK: Yes, but it is a form of variation that would have been inconceivable without atonality and serialism, atonality being a necessary assumption, because the simultaneities of sounds unpredictably resulting from the chance operations will be acceptable only in atonality, and because serialism offers the cues for those operations.

WO: Have advanced stages of predetermined serialism, such as that of *Quaestio Temporis,* raised the ante, so to speak, on communicating or perceiving musical "thoughts"?

EK: To ears and minds attuned to the traditional concepts of theme and development serial music may indeed cause some difficulties of perception. This music does not seem any longer to move from point to point, from a clear beginning to an end that is seen as the consummation of a thought process, but its constituent elements are rather perceived as solid or even elastic objects set up against each other in spatial relationships. I have noticed that some specimens of later serial, or perhaps post-serial music have a very pronounced static character. Now, accepting or rejecting this may be entirely a question of taste, for there is no law prohibiting music from being static. But I wonder whether nearly completely giving up linear design may not be too high a price to pay for developing the new static image, for it seems that many of the so-conceived compositions fail to sustain the listeners' attention, especially if they become as long as some of the younger composers appear to be inclined to make them. In some of these works I seem to detect a sort of neoprimitivism, which reminds me of the situation of the mid-eighteenth century when "progressive" or "modern" meant to be childishly simple. But spurning the awesome involutions of late Bach was probably the corollary for gaining any new territory at all.

WO: Some of the early tillers of the soil of serialism have now abandoned those fields. Are you planning to do so?

EK: I remember having said some twenty or more years ago that I thought the twelve-tone technique would become, for those who have gone through its strictures, a kind of second nature so that they would be able to write music of a dodecaphonic character without having to employ the mechanics of this discipline. I think that this applies to serialism as well. Personally, I do not think that the potentialities of serial procedure are exhausted, and I am still deriving much satisfaction from employing it off and on in various degrees. My impression is that some composers who have abandoned serial discipline try to overcome the dangers of static stagnation through increased emphasis on sensational sound qualities, or other features that might be called gimmicks—by which I mean tricks that are designed to attract attention to nothing but themselves, similar to what Richard Wagner called "effects without cause."

WO: Do you include contemporary "collage" pieces among these?

EK: I am afraid that the few specimens I know belong there. They also are apt to arouse the suspicion that the authors are trying to ride on some celebrities coattails, which presumably was not their intention.

WO: And how do you regard graphic music and similar notational experiments?

EK: Again I feel that some of these endeavors touch upon gimmickry, since the unfamiliar and often very involved symbols make grasping the composer's ideas more difficult, slow, and uncertain, rather than facilitating them which in my opinion should be the ultimate purpose of any kind of notation. I apply this criticism also to some of the elaborate prefaces and instructions we find in so many new scores because they are more likely to befuddle the reader than to tell him in generally understandable technical language how to go about playing the music.

WO: In your book *Music Here and Now* you prophesied a future in which one might compose music by writing directly on sound track. Wouldn't this have resulted in a graphic score?

EK: Not exactly, since the lines drawn onto the sound track would not be graphic symbols of sounds, but sounds themselves translated into a different medium and activated by light. I understand that this idea was later carried out experimentally here and there. Of course this method has become obsolete through the rapid development of electronic musicmaking.

WO: What attracted you especially to the electronic medium when you started working in it on your oratorio-type composition *Spiritus intelligentiae, sanctus*?

EK: At that time I began to delve into the problems of serialism and was fascinated by the unlimited possibilities of the electronic technique for extreme rhythmic subtlety, such as seemed to be indispensable in serial composition.

With serialism coming of age, painstakingly computed rhythmic complexity does not any longer seem to be a goal so insistently to be pursued as it was twenty or so years ago. Thus the cutting and splicing of tapes to the millimeter is not any longer required in order to realize the composer's ideas. Fortunately, it is technically no longer necessary either. Curiously enough, the electronic medium, earlier denounced as a mechanistic degradation of music, lends itself to a kind of controlled compositional improvisation much more readily than the realm of live sound because the composer can mold the sound material while he is creating it.

As I see it, there is a danger in this situation, and some composers, especially beginners, fall prey to it. They become so infatuated with the material aspects of the medium, with the novelty of the sounds they are able to coax out of the apparatus, that they forget to compose music. By "compose" I do not mean employing the traditional developmental procedures, but creating some sort of design that will hold the listener's interest.

WO: Does the coming of age of electronics tempt you to abandon live performance?

EK: On the contrary, I think that the combination of electronic sounds with vocal and instrumental resources offers fascinating possibilities. Earlier experiments in this direction were not very successful, but this is plausible enough since one had to deal with entirely unknown quantities and qualities. Compositions of this kind are, in terms of social relations, no different from the traditional type. Purely electronic works will probably find a more adequate response, when they are listened to privately by small groups of individuals, coming over the radio or the speaker of a tape recorder. Sitting in a large hall and staring at an empty platform while being besieged by the sounds scattered around by a battery of loudspeakers is usually a depressing experience.

WO: You don't seem to hold this opinion alone. But what of the recent environments in Europe and Japan that immerse the visitor in a continuous sound bath along with other sensory stimuli for as long as he wanders through the maze of the environment? What do you think of such efforts?

EK: It sounds somehow familiar to me. We have had it in this country for a long time. We call it Muzak.

APPENDIX

ABBREVIATIONS FOR NAMES OF PUBLISHERS

A	Hermann Assmann, Frankfurt/M, Germany
AMP	Associated Music Publishers, New York
BV	Bärenreiter Verlag, Kassel, Germany
BM	Belwin Mills, New York
BB	Broude Brothers, New York
D	Ludwig Doblinger, Vienna, Austria
GI	Gregorian Institute, Toledo, Ohio
H	Wilhelm Hansen, Copenhagen, Denmark
M	E. B. Marks, New York
Me	Mercury Music, New York
P	O. Pagani, New York
Schi	G. Schirmer, New York
Scho	B. Schott's Sohne, Main, Germany
So	Southern Music, New York
UE	Universal Edition, Vienna, Austria

Appendix

LIST OF ERNST KRENEK'S MUSICAL AND LITERARY WORKS

Opus Number[1]	*Title and Year of Origin*	*Publisher*
	I. OPERAS	
14	Zwingburg (The Tyrant's Castle) 1922	UE
17	Der Sprung über den Schatten (The Leap Over the Shadow) 1923	UE
21	Orpheus und Eurydike (Oskar Kokoschka) 1923	UE
37	Mammon (ballet) (Béla Balasz) 1925	UE
45	Jonny spielt auf (Jonny strikes up) 1925	UE
49	Der Diktator (The Dictator) 1926	UE
50	Das geheime Königreich (The Secret Kingdom) 1927	UE
55	Schwergewicht oder Die Ehre der Nation (Heavyweight or The Pride of the Nation) 1927	UE

[1] A few numbers are missing. These were applied to works later withdrawn by the composer or to works he regards as of lesser significance.

Opus Number	*Title and Year of Origin*	*Publisher*
60	Leben des Orest (Life of Orestes) 1929	UE
73	Karl V (Charles V) 1933	UE
77	Cefalo e Procri (Cephalus and Procris) (Rinaldo Küfferle) 1934	UE
90	Tarquin (Emmet Lavery) 1940	
111	What Price Confidence? 1945	BV
125	Dark Waters 1950	BV
144	Pallas Athene weint (Pallas Athena Weeps) 1955	Scho/UE
153	The Bell Tower (after Herman Melville)	BV
179	Ausgerechnet und verspielt 1961	BV
186	Der goldene Bock (The Golden Ram) 1963	BV
192	Der Zauberspiegel (The Magic Mirror) 1966	BV
206	Sardakai 1969	BV
217	Flaschenpost vom Paradies (Bottled Message from Paradise) TV play 1973	

Librettos by the composer unless indicated differently

II. ORCHESTRAL WORKS

7	First Symphony 1921	UE
11	Symphonic Music f. 9 instr. 1922	UE
12	Second Symphony 1922	UE
16	Third Symphony 1922	UE
18	First Piano Concerto 1923	UE
25	Concerto grosso 1924	UE
27	Concertino (flute, violin, harpsichord, strings) 1924	UE
29	First Violin Concerto 1924	UE
31	Seven Orchestra Pieces 1924	UE

Opus Number	*Title and Year of Origin*	*Publisher*
34	Symphony f. wind instr. and percussion 1925	UE
43	Suite f. small orch. 1927	UE
44	Three Marches f. wind instr. 1926	UE
54	Potpourri 1927	UE
58	Little Symphony 1928	UE
69	Theme and 13 variations 1931	UE
70a	Little Wind Music (orch. version of Piano 70)	UE
80	Campo Marzio, overture 1937	UE
81	Second Piano Concerto 1937	UE
86	Symphonic Piece f. String Orch. 1939	Scho/UE
88	Little Concerto f. organ, harpsichord and small orch. 1940	
94	I Wonder as I Wander, variations 1942	
101	Tricks and Trifles (orch. version of Piano 100) 1945	
105	Symphonic Elegy f. string orch. 1946	BM
107	Third Piano Concerto 1946	Scho/UE
113	Fourth Symphony 1947	
116	Five Pieces f. strings 1948	
119	Fifth Symphony 1949	Scho/UE
123	Fourth Piano Concerto 1950	BV
124	Double Concerto f. Violin, Piano and chamber orch. 1950	UE
126	Concerto f. Harp and chamber orch. 1951	UE
127	Concerto f. 2 Pianos 1951	BV
131	Sinfonietta "A Brasileira" f. string orch.	UE
133	Violoncello Concerto 1953	BV
134	Scenes from the West (4 pieces f. school orch.)	BM

Opus Number	*Title and Year of Origin*	*Publisher*
137	Symphony "Pallas Athene" 1954	Scho/UE
140	Second Violin Concerto 1954	Scho/UE
142	Eleven Transparencies 1954	Scho/UE
145	Cappriccio f. Violoncello and chamber orch. 1955	Scho/UE
146	Seven Easy Pieces f. string orch. 1955	Scho
147a	Suite f. Flute and string. orch. (see IV. Chamber Music, 147) 1954	BB
148a	Suite f. Clarinet and string orch. (see IV. Chamber Music, 148) 1955	BB
160	Kette, Kreis und Spiegel (Circle, Chain and Mirror) 1957	BV
162	Marginal Sounds f. Perc. etc.	BB
167	Hexahedron (6 pieces f. chamber orch.) 1958	
170	Quaestio temporis (A Question of Time) 1959	BV
177	From Three Make Seven 1961	BV
182	Nach wie vor der Reihe nach (Serially as before) f. orch. with 2 speakers 1962	BV
196	Horizon Circled 1967	BV
199	Perspectives 1967	BV
200	Exercises of a Late Hour (with electr. tape) 1967	BV
203	Six Profiles 1968	BV
205	Fivefold Enfoldment 1969	BV
213	Kitharaulos f. Oboe, Harp and chamber orch. 1972	BV
214	Static and Ecstatic 1972	BV

III. VOCAL MUSIC[1]

1. SOLO VOICES

a) with piano

Opus Number	*Title and Year of Origin*	*Publisher*
9, 15, 19, 30	Songs (G. H. Goering, F. Werfel, O. Krzyzanowski, H. Reinhart) 1921–1924	UE (partly)
48	O Lacrymosa (R. M. Rilke) 1926	UE
53	Four Songs (Baroque poetry) 1927	UE
56	Three Songs (Goethe) 1927	UE
57	Stella's Monologue (Goethe) 1928	UE
62	Reisebuch aus den österreichischen Alpen (Journey through the Austrian Alps) 1929	UE
64	Fiedellieder (Fiddle Songs) (Th. Storm, Th. Mommsen) 1930	UE
67	Durch die Nacht (Through the Night) (Karl Kraus) 1931	UE
68	Die Nachtigall (The Nightingale) (Karl Kraus) 1931	UE
71	Gesange des späten Jahres (Songs of the Late Year) 1931	UE
75	Das Schweigen (Silence) (Gemmingen)	
76	Während der Trennung (During Separation) (Fleming)	
82	Five Songs (F. Kafka) 1938	Scho/UE
84a	The Night is Far Spent (Saint Paul) 1939	Schi
98	The Ballad of the Railroads 1944	BV
104	Etude f. Contralto and Coloratura-Soprano (a cappella) 1945	

[1] Where no authors are listed, the words are by the composer.

Opus Number	*Title and Year of Origin*	*Publisher*
112	Four Songs (G. M. Hopkins) 1947	BV
132	Two Sacred Songs (Bible) 1952	BV
175	The Flea (J. Donne) 1960	M
189	Wechselrahmen (Changing Frame) (E. Barth) 1965	BV
216	Three Songs (L. Sauter) 1972	
218	Spätlese (Late Harvest) 1973	

b) with instrumental groups

30a	Three Songs (E. Verhaeren) 1924	
48a	O Lacrymosa (see above)	UE
53a	Four Songs (see above)	UE
67a	Durch die Nacht (see above)	UE
68a	Die Nachtigall (The Nightingale) (see above)	UE
91	La Corona f. Mezzo-Sopr., Baritone, Organ, and Perc. (J. Donne) 1941	BV
91a	The Holy Ghost's Ark (J. Donne) 1941	
161	Sestina f. Sopr. and 10 players 1957	BV
191	Quintina f. Sopr., 6 players and electr. tape 1965	BV
201	Instant remembered f. Sopr. and small orch. (E. Krenek, Seneca, G. M. Hopkins, K. Kraus) 1968	BV

c) with orchestra

57a	Monologue of Stella (Sopr.) (see above)	UE
73a	Fragments from Charles V (Sopr.)	UE
129	Medea (R. Jeffers after Euripides) (Sopr.) 1952	BV

Opus Number	*Title and Year of Origin*	*Publisher*
	2. CHORAL MUSIC	
22	Three choruses a capp. (M. Claudius) 1923	UE
32	Four small choruses (men's voices a capp. with contralto solo) (F. Hölderlin) 1924	UE
35	The Seasons (a capp.) (F. Hölderlin) 1925	UE
47	Four choruses a capp. (Goethe) 1926	UE
61	Three choruses a capp. (G. Keller) 1929	UE
72	Cantata on the Transitoriness of Earthly Things (f. mixed chorus, sopr. solo and piano) (Baroque poetry) 1932	UE
74	Jagd im Winter (Hunt in Winter) (F. Grillparzer) 1933	
77a	Four Austrian Folksongs (arr.) 1934	UE
87	Two choruses f. women's voices a capp. (W. Drummond, Sir Walter Raleigh) 1939	BB
89	Proprium Missae f. SS. Innocents' Day, f. women's voices a capp. (Bible) 1940	BM
93	Lamentatio Jeremiae Prophetae (Bible), f. mixed chorus a capp. 1941	BV
95	Cantata for Wartime f. women's voices and orch. (H. Melville) 1944	Scho/UE
97	Five Prayers f. women's voices a capp. (J. Donne) 1944	UE
102	The Santa Fe Timetable f. mixed chorus a capp. (Santa Fe Railroad) 1945	BV
103	Aegrotavit Ezechias f. 3 women's voices and piano (Bible) 1945	
106	In Paradisum f. women's voices a capp. (Bible) 1945	BB

Opus Number	*Title and Year of Origin*	*Publisher*
109	O Would I Were f. mixed chorus a capp. (anon.) 1946	Me
115a	Remember Now f. women's voices and piano (Bible) 1947	
138a-d	Four choruses f. mixed voices and organ (Bible) 1953	BM
143	Proprium Missae in Domenica III in Quadragesima f. 3 mixed voices a capp. (Bible) 1954	Scho
141	Veni Sanctificator (as above) 1954	Scho
149	Psalm Verses (as above) 1955	Scho
151	I Sing Again, f. mixed chorus and strings (W.v.d. Vogelweide) 1956	Scho/UE
159	Good Morning, America, f. mixed chorus a capp. (C. Sandburg) 1956	Scho
165	Missa Duodecim Tonorum f. mixed chorus and organ 1958	GI
169	Six Motets, f. mixed chorus a capp. (F. Kafka) 1959	BV
174	Three Madrigals and Three Motets f. children's voices (misc. texts) 1960	BB
181	Canon f. Igor Stravinsky's 80th birthday f. 2 mixed voices 1962	BV
186a	O Holy Ghost, f. mixed chorus a capp. (J. Donne) 1964	BV
194	Glauben und Wissen (To believe and to know) f. mixed chorus and orch. 1966	
195	Proprium for Trinitatis, f. sopr. solo, mixed chorus and instr. 1967	BV
202	Proprium for St. Mary's Nativity, f. solo voice, mixed chorus and instr. (in Catalan language) 1968	

Opus Number	*Title and Year of Origin*	*Publisher*
204	Deutsche Messe (German Mass) f. solo voices, mixed chorus and instr. 1968	BV
208	Messe "Gib uns den Frieden" (Mass 'Give us our peace') f. solo voices, mixed chorus and instr. 1970	BV
210	Three Sacred Pieces and Three Lessons, f. mixed chorus a capp. 1971	BB

IV. CHAMBER MUSIC

4	Serenade f. Clar., Violin, Viola and 'cello 1919	A
6	First String Quartet 1921	UE
8	Second String Quartet 1921	A
20	Third String Quartet 1923	UE
24	Fourth String Quartet 1924	
28	Little Suite f. Clarinet and Piano 1924	BV
65	Fifth String Quartet 1930	UE
78	Sixth String Quartet 1936	UE
85a	Themes by Handel, f. Oboe and Piano	BM
85b	Country Dance, f. 4 Clar. 1939	BM
85c	Fluteplayers' Serenade, f. 4 Flutes	BM
85d	Sonatina f. Bass Clarinet and Piano	BM
92/2b	Sonatina f. Flute and Clarinet (or Viola) 1942	BV
96	Seventh String Quartet 1944	UE
99	Sonata f. Violin and Piano 1945	UE
108	Trio f. Clar., Violin and Piano 1946	AMP
117	Sonata f. Viola and Piano 1948	BM
118	String Trio 1949	H
122	Parvula Corona ad honorem J. S. Bach, f. String Trio 1950	

Opus Number	*Title and Year of Origin*	*Publisher*
135	Phantasiestück f. 'cello and Piano 1953	
147	Suite f. Flute and Piano (same as Orch. 147a)	BB
148	Suite f. Clar. and Piano (same as Orch. 148a)	BB
163	Pentagram f. 5 wind instr. 1957	BV
171	Flute Piece in 9 Phases, with Piano 1959	BV
172	Hausmusik (7 pieces for the 7 days of the week, f. several instr.) 1959	BV
180	Alpbach Quintet, f. 5 wind instr. 1962	UE
187	Fibonacci-Mobile, f. String quartet and Piano 4 hds. 1964	BV
193	Four Pieces f. Oboe and Piano 1966	BV
198	Five Pieces f. Trombone and Piano 1967	BV
209	Duo f. Flute and Contrabass 1970	
213	Aulokithara f. Oboe, Harp and electr. tape (arr. from Orch. 213) 1972	BV

V. SOLO INSTRUMENTS

1. VARIOUS INSTRUMENTS

156	Oboe: Sonatina 1956	BB
157	Clarinet: Monologue 1956	BB
150	Harp: Sonata 1955	BV
183	Accordion: Toccata 1962	P
164	Guitar: Suite 1957	D
92	Organ: Sonata 1941	BM
180½	Organologia 1962	
212	Orga-Nastro (with electr. tape) 1971	BV
33	Violin: First Sonata 1925	A
115	Violin: Second Sonata 1948	

Opus Number	*Title and Year of Origin*	*Publisher*
92/3	Viola: Sonata 1942	Schi
84	Violoncello: Suite 1939	Schi

2. PIANO

Opus Number	*Title and Year of Origin*	*Publisher*
1a	Double Fugue 1918	
1b	Dance Study 1920	UE
2	First Sonata 1919	UE
5	Five Sonatinas 1920	
13	Toccata and Chaconne 1922	UE
13a	Little Suite (appendix to 13) 1922	UE
26	Two Suites 1924	UE
39	Five Pieces 1925	UE
59	Second Sonata 1928	UE/AMP
70	Four Bagatelles, or Sonata (4 hds.) 1931	
79	Twelve Variations 1937	A
83	Twelve Short Pieces 1938	Schi
92/4	Third Sonata 1943	AMP
100	Hurricane Variations 1944	
110	Eight Pieces 1946	Me
114	Fourth Sonata 1948	Schi
120	George Washington Variations 1950	So
121	Fifth Sonata 1950	
128	Sixth Sonata 1951	
136	Twenty Miniatures 1954	H
166	Echoes from Austria (arr. Austrian folksongs) 1958	BB
168	Sechs Vermessene (Six measured, or presuming items) 1958	BV
173	Basler Massarbeit (Basle custom made) f. 2 pianos 1958	BV
197	Piano Piece in eleven parts 1967	

Opus Number	Title and Year of Origin	Publisher
207	Doppelt beflügeltes Band (Tape and Doubles) f. 2 pianos and electr. tape 1970	BV

VI. ELECTRONIC MUSIC

152	Spiritus intelligentiae, sanctus (with voices) (Bible) 1956	UE
185	San Fernando Sequence 1963	
190	Quintona 1965	

VII. SPECIAL ITEMS

18a	Completion of an unfinished Piano Sonata in C-major by Franz Schubert 1922	UE
80a	arr. L'incoronazione di Poppea, opera by Claudio Monteverdi 1936	UE
80b	Suite from 80a, f. orch. 1937	UE

VIII. BOOKS

Über neue Musik (On New Music) 1936	Vienna 1937
Music Here and Now 1938	New York 1939 and 1967
Studies in Counterpoint based on the twelve-tone technique 1939	New York 1940
Hamline Studies in Musicology (ed. by E. K.)	St. Paul, Minn. 1945–1947
Selbstdarstellung 1948	Zurich 1948
Self-analysis (Engl. transl. of preceding in New Mexico Quarterly, Spring 1953)	
Musik im goldenen Westen (Music in the Golden West) 1949	Vienna 1949

Johannes Ockeghem 1952	New York 1953
Modal Counterpoint 1953	New York 1959
Tonal Counterpoint 1953	New York 1958
De rebus prius factis 1956	Copenhagen 1956
Zur Sprache gebracht (Given Word) (Selected essays)	Munich 1958
Gedanken unterwegs (Thoughts Along the Way) (selected essays)	Munich 1959
Prosa, Dramen, Verse (Fiction, theatrical works, poetry selection)	Munich 1965
Exploring Music (Engl. version of a selection from Zur Sprache gebracht)	London 1966